A GLOBAL CALL TO PRAYER

Intercession in Action

Blessings!
Germaine Copeland

By

Germaine Copeland

Harrison House

Tulsa, OK

15 14 13 12 11 10   9 8 7 6 5 4 3 2 1

A Global Call to Prayer:
Intercession in Action
ISBN 10: 1-60683-012-0
ISBN 13: 978-1-60683-012-3
Copyright © 2010 by Germaine Copeland
1140 Brannon Drive
Greensboro, Georgia 30642

Published by Harrison House Publishers
P.O. Box 35035
Tulsa, Oklahoma 74153
www.harrisonhouse.com

CONTENTS

INTRODUCTION

THEN HE showed me the river whose waters give life, sparkling like crystal, flowing out from the throne of God and of the Lamb. Through the middle of the broadway of the city; also, on either side of the river was the tree of life with its twelve varieties of fruit, yielding each month its fresh crop; and the leaves of the tree were for the healing *and* the restoration of the nations.

—Revelation 22:1-2 AMP

The prayer team was in the exotic and colorful nation of Morocco known in Arabic as the Maghreb, "the place where the sun sets." We had been touring for several days, and were excited about returning to a village we had visited earlier. After a few hours our host and driver pulled into a parking space and we hurriedly made our way through the downtown streets. There was so much to see: stalls with fresh meats hanging up, fruits, vegetables, and so much more. There were people everywhere. Some were sitting at the outside café tables drinking coffee or mint tea; women were shopping; and smiling merchants were standing outside their stalls beckoning us to come in. Trying not to stare, we looked into the faces of young girls and women, some with veils. They avoided making eye contact, but often they smiled. I prayed the light in our eyes would rejoice the hearts of all those we met, and I wished I could talk with them: *"for the healing and the restoration of the nations"* (v. 22:2 AMP).

Leaving the village behind, our host and driver wended his way up the mountain road where we were free to pray. A November mist draped itself over us as we responded to the grace of God that had called us here to pray and demonstrate His love to some of the most hospitable people I had ever met.

Just as the prayer team began to pray for the people of this nation, we heard the eerie sound of the Muslim call to prayer filling the air. Faithful men came from all sections of the town and entered the mosque for the mid-afternoon prayers. According to their tradition they knelt in respectful reference to pray. I thought of our host who requested we pray for the Imams; pray for the leaders of the areas where we visited. Lord, fill our hearts with the fire of Your love, and let me see with Your eyes of love and compassion.

In one place where we stayed, we saw a man kneeling on a prayer rug provided by the Hotel for daily prayers. We could learn something about reverence from the people of this land. A thought flashes through my mind: *How long has it been since I knelt before the Lord, my God, as I was taught to do as a young child. Could it be that*

I and many in the Church have thrown away those acts of reverence in favor of "freedom?" I am concerned for America. The reverence for God and for the Bible seems to have diminished.

Driving through large cities and small town USA you find churches; rural churches tucked away in grassy pastures, uptown churches on street corners. You don't have to drive far to find a church building, yet is still seems we have not learned to love one another. There is life in the prayer closet that prepares us to live outside the prayer closet, to love others as Jesus loves. He prayed we would be a people united, that we would be one even as He and the Father are one. (John 17.) He gave us one commandment: love one another as I have loved you.[1] Where there is harmony and unity there is answered prayer. We have been born for such a time as this…a time when the followers of Jesus are coming together to pray in agreement with the Word of God. My prayer is for the Father to open our eyes and give us insight into His purposes and plans—to help us see beyond our natural eyes. Where do we go from here? *Lord Jesus, help us to fulfill Your Word and reach the many souls waiting for the united prayers of Your people! Let us be the glorious church of salt and light: "That he might present it to himself a glorious church, not having spot, or wrinkle, or any such thing; but that it should be holy and without blemish" (Ephesians 5:27).*

The nations of our world need healing today. In the kindergarten years of the classroom of prayer, while the warm sunshine beamed on the bedroom floor where I was kneeling, I saw a parade of people dressed in the native clothing of the nations of the world. It was God's way of showing me that He has called His people to pray for the nations of the world. As I observed the parade of people a love for each one radiated from within me. My prayer journey began that day.

Why pray and does prayer make a difference? This book is written to encourage you to know God, His thoughts and His ways, and to participate with Jesus in His present-day ministry of intercessory prayer. Those who intercede effectively for the nations are people who have knowledge, sound judgment, and they are teachable. Do not fear making a mistake and always exchange error for truth.

With the help of my prayer group I wrote a series of books, *Prayers That Avail Much*®, which are filled with powerful Scriptural prayers. We found that praying in line with what the Bible says is effective. It is God's Word and His Will. You will find some of these prayers in this book, but I encourage you to seek the Scriptures for yourself. My prayer group and I have an intense desire to be controlled by the Holy Spirit who knows what to pray when we don't. He knows the will of the Father. An effective intercessor studies the Scriptures; he looks to the Word of God for direction, guidance, sound doctrine, reproof, correction and instruction. (2 Timothy 3:16.)

Prayer is about relationship, communication with God. There are people who want to learn how to pray for the purpose of getting God to do their bidding, but the ultimate purpose is to receive and know God who is Love. His love teaches us who we are in Christ and our place in God's economy. The archenemy understands the importance of prayer, and works diligently to distract us—to rob us of time and energy we would give to prayer. If he can't stop us from praying, he tries to keep our focus on our needs and problems rather than on the eternal God of heaven and earth.

It is amazing to me the Creator involves us in His plan for humanity, even calling us His co-laborers. Remember, there is no distance in the spirit world. That prayer you offer up in your present location can strike like lightning in another part of the world, bringing about the plan and purpose of God.

When you begin to pray for others, you are participating in the present-day ministry of Jesus Christ, "He always lives to make intercession for them" (Hebrews 7:25 NKJV). By the grace of God we answer the call to pray, and through prayer, we become His voice in the earth. With the help of the Holy Spirit, we learn how to become effective co-laborers with our heavenly Father.

It is my intention in these pages to share with you some insights the Holy Spirit has taught me over the past several years about the subject of prayer. Although much of my training was while praying for family situations, these principles apply to all prayer assignments. (In fact, praying for your family may be the toughest prayer assignment you will ever have because you have to allow the Holy Spirit to deal with areas of personal unhealed emotional hurts, unresolved issues, soulish desires, and motives.)

Even though I share personal experiences and some truths with you in this book, the only way you will ever really learn about prayer is to actively get involved in it yourself. It is then your personal Teacher and Guide, the Holy Spirit, gives you wisdom and spiritual understanding in this vital area. Prayer becomes a joy and an adventure as you learn to hear the Holy Spirit.

I have no formulas to offer, only truths the Holy Spirit has imparted as I set my face like flint to seek first the Kingdom of God and His righteousness. It has been said we will have no desire to pray apart from the grace He gives so we can't pat ourselves on the back and say, "Look what I have done." It's all for His glory and honor, but we receive the victory—answered prayer.

God looks for those *who will build up the wall and stand in the gap before Him for the land (family, government, community) that He should not destroy it* (Ezekiel 22:30). When I began to ask the Holy Spirit to teach me to pray effectively for our son's deliverance from a lifestyle of addiction, one of the first lessons He taught me was that I was not alone. God had other intercessors He called to pray for our family who did not know us personally and together we saw the salvation of the Lord. From that experience I learned not only does God tell us in His Word *how* to pray, He also tells us *who* is called to pray, and *the way* to enter into this important phase of our walk in the Spirit.

Today, our world is in crisis, and we need divine intervention. God gives prayer strategy and equips His "co-laborers" to move in and out of the world systems, the mountains of media, government, business, religion, family, education, and entertainment. He intends for the Body of Christ to take charge of these societal structures or "gates of society" through prayer for the purpose of bringing reformation to our world. This requires prayer by those who are willing to build up the wall and stand in the gap before Him for the nations of the world.

Sometimes I wonder if we here in America think we are God's favored ones when the Scriptures clearly reveal God loves the world (John 3:16), and that includes those *far away places with strange sounding names*. The names are becoming more familiar to us day by day. I pray that this book will inspire you to expand your prayer life to include others outside your own family, community, and region.

For the earth shall be filled with the knowledge of
the glory of the LORD, as the waters cover the sea.

Habakkuk 2:14

CHAPTER 1
A GLOBAL CALL TO PRAYER

A young mother had been attending the Bible study for several weeks. I noticed the stern look on her face when she rushed up to me after class one day. "If we believe what you teach we will have to pray for the whole world." Yes, but we as one body can do it as the Lord leads us. In the book of Isaiah we find that to the Lord: "The nations are like a drop from a bucket and are counted as small dust on the scales; behold, He takes up the isles like a very little thing" (Isaiah 40:15 AMP). The Lord is not intimidated by the world's problems. He knows when we pray, things change. We may be concerned about environmental disasters, the poor in third world countries, incurable disease, and a host of other problems but one of the most important things we can do is come together and take these seemingly insurmountable challenges before the Lord in prayer. Let's see how Jesus did this when He walked the earth.

JESUS PRAYS FOR HIS CHURCH

That they all may be one; as thou, Father, *art* in me, and I in thee, that they also may be one in us: that the world may believe that thou hast sent me. And the glory which thou gavest me I have given them; *that they may be one, even as we are one*: I in them, and thou in me, that they may be made perfect in one; and that the world may know that thou hast sent me, and hast loved them, as thou hast loved me.

John 17:21-23

This love Jesus refers to is the unity of the Body of Christ; the reality of this Scripture is rooted and grounded in love as described in First Corinthians, the thirteenth chapter. Let unity begin with us in our prayer closets. If we pray in secret the Father will reward us openly in our communications and relationships.[2] He will heal our land.

"What the world needs now is love, sweet love…that's the only thing there is just too little of"[3] plays round and round in my head. Love has come; Love hung on a cross and yet so many seem unaware. With blinded eyes they fail to see they are loved unconditionally. It's almost a fairy tale, except fairy tales aren't true. God, Who created all things, came to earth as a vulnerable Infant became sin with our sin and suffered the punishment for mankind. We've a Story to Tell to the Nations![4] There are those who go and tell the story and there are those who stay behind praying. We are one body.

The entire Church must answer the call to pray for the nations and be willing to stand for righteousness even when it isn't popular. A revival and spiritual revolution will require of us to live truly, deal truly, and speak truly. Are we ready to lead the country and run our businesses and homes as Jesus would? What will it cost you to take up your cross and follow Him? Love. Love for humanity. You may have to change the way you do business; you may have to become a statesman rather than a politician with a personal agenda. What would Jesus do in your situation? Love must rule in our hearts.

STAND IN THE GAP

God is a God of justice, mercy, grace, strength, power, might, love, and righteousness. In Ezekiel 22:30, God looked for an intercessor who would stand before Him on behalf of Israel so He would not have to pour out His indignation upon them and consume them with the fire of His wrath. When I read the entire chapter where Israel's sins are listed, I shudder. It sounds like the world we live in.

God has already judged sin, and it seems America is running recklessly away from God who is looking for His intercessors to stand before Him on behalf of the nations.

"I looked for a man among them who would build up the wall and stand before me in the gap on behalf of the land so I would not have to destroy it, but I found none.

So I will pour out my wrath on them and consume them

with my fiery anger, bringing down on their own heads

all they have done, declares the Sovereign LORD."

Ezekiel 22:30-31 NIV

Again, I emphasize, this is a call to you and me as part of the Church to unite with others, lay aside our differences, and come together on the basis of our faith in Jesus Christ. Wake up, O Church and take God at His Word as He says in Psalms: "Ask of Me, and I will give You the nations as Your inheritance, and the uttermost parts of the earth as Your possession" (2:8 AMP).

Intercession can change nations and the lives of individuals. There are churches across America of all denominations, some mega churches, some small. Television and radio have many ministers who preach the Gospel of Jesus Christ. God has imparted to the Church the awesome power that raised Jesus from the dead; He declares us more than conquerors and overcomers in this world.[5] Yet, here in America evil is being called good and good, evil. America hears the Gospel but it still needs our prayers. How much more is there a need for prayer in the nations of the world where the Gospel is not preached?

It is my prayer God will open your mind and heart to hear the cry that is being released in the heavens...a cry for freedom, a cry for justice, a cry for peace. Listen to the screams of those who are being tortured...hear the prayers of the martyrs. They are our brothers and sisters. You may never go to a nation outside your own borders, except while in your personal prayer closet but how valuable are those prayers. This is a call to you, the Church of the Lord Jesus Christ, to awaken to the heart cry of the Father in John 3:16: "For God so loved the world, that he gave his only begotten Son, that whosoever believeth in him should not perish, but have everlasting life."

Jesus' Desire to Pray for the Nations

Go with me back to the days when Jesus walked the earth, in Mark's Gospel, chapter eleven. Join me with the crowd following Jesus.

Listen to the cries of the people! I hurry to catch up and hear, "Hosanna! Praise to the One who comes in the Name of the Lord." I weave my way in and out of the crowd to be near to Jesus and His disciples. As we approach the temple, the atmosphere of the crowd is quiet and I wonder what is happening when I see Jesus entering the temple where He looks around; His expression serious and sorrowful. Suddenly, Jesus and His group turn. They are walking away and I have to run to catch up, and continue following them all the way to Bethany where they settle down for the night. I find a spot where I feel safe and fall asleep.

Awaking to the noises around me I jump up from my hiding place, eating the crust of bread and drinking the water which I carry at my side. I have to hurry to keep up with Jesus and His disciples. In Jerusalem I follow closely and manage to enter the temple with them. Then it happens! Anger I've never known resonates through the temple and the people are speechless for a moment. Then bedlam is all around me, men screaming and yelling trying to protect their merchandise. Jesus has turned the tables over and is driving the vendors from the temple area! He has managed to block the entrance of those who try to use the temple as a shortcut. Vendors are yelling, turtledoves flying away, coins clanging and rolling around! I am frozen to the place where I stand wondering if I should help the vendors or walk away with Jesus and His company. I must be dreaming! Before I know it, I am in the pack that is following Jesus outside the temple area, and suddenly we all come to a halt.

Standing on tiptoes I look to see why we have stopped; I see Jesus. People sit down on the grass to listen to what He is saying. Shortly, I realize He is teaching from a Scripture in Isaiah we had heard from the rabbis. I can't believe what He is saying about the temple…He's calling it a temple for all nations. Surely He will overthrow the Roman government and set the Jewish people free from tyranny! Indignant, I silently scream, *We are the chosen people!* Could it be that we are to really pray for all men everywhere? God is interested in the healing of the nations?

And they came to Jerusalem. And He went into the temple [area, the porches and courts] and began to drive out those who sold and bought in the temple area, and He overturned the [four-footed] tables of the money changers and the seats of those who dealt in doves; And He would not permit anyone to carry any household equipment through the temple enclosure [thus making the temple area a short-cut traffic lane]. And He taught and said to them, Is it not written, My house shall be called a house of prayer for *all the nations?* But you have turned it into a den of robbers.

Mark 11:15-17 AMP

Matthew and Mark recorded this so we wouldn't forget what the Messiah taught us. This message is passed down through the centuries to every believer. The disciples of Jesus recognize the secret of His power is prayer. They don't ask Him to teach them how to do miracles, but ask Him to teach them to pray. (Luke 11.)

WE ARE THE CHILDREN OF LIGHT

Not only has Jesus taught us to pray, but He says He is sending us a Helper who will help us pray when we don't know how to produce results. This divine Helper is here on earth to help us pray effectively and He knows the mind of the Father. (Romans 8) The time has come for the Body of Christ to arise from our slumber. As the darkness grows darker, the light will shine brighter. We are the children of Light! In the book of Isaiah, notice how the nations are drawn to the children of Light:

ARISE [from the depression and prostration in which circumstances have kept you—rise to a new life]! Shine (be radiant with the glory of the Lord), for your light has come, and the glory of the Lord has risen upon you! For behold, darkness shall cover the earth, and dense darkness [all] peoples, but the Lord shall arise upon you [O Jerusalem], and His glory shall be seen on you. And nations shall come to your light, and kings to the brightness of your rising.

Isaiah 60:1-3 AMP

Let's be willing to put away our differences, our dogmas and *arise!* The god of this world and the circumstances in which we live are not greater than our God and His glory is to be seen. The time is here for revival. The Father, by His grace, will create within us a willing heart, and we will take up our cross and follow Jesus.

Our Light has come and we are the light of the world. It's time to come out from under the bushel, and cast off the weights that so easily beset us; our light is to shine into the recesses of a crooked and perverse generation. Let us examine ourselves. Have we conformed so much to the culture of our nation that we are comfortable in our circumstances? Jesus said to "let your light so shine before men that they may see your moral excellence and your praiseworthy, noble, and good deeds and recognize, and honor and praise and glorify your Father Who is in heaven" (Matthew 5:16 AMP). If we want our intercession to be effective we should desire to live as it becomes children of God, as imitators of Him, or we lose our saltiness and the light will go out in our communities and nation. My everyday-going-to-work life should be compatible with my prayers.

> The Earth is the Lord's, and the fullness of it, the world and they who dwell in it. For He has founded it upon the seas and established it upon the currents *and* the rivers. Who shall go up into the mountain of the Lord? Or who shall stand in His Holy Place? He who has clean hands and a pure heart, who has not lifted himself up to falsehood *or* to what is false, nor sworn deceitfully.
>
> Psalm 24:1-4 AMP

When we pray according to the will of God we enter into the present-day ministry of Jesus who is seated at the right of the Father interceding. This demands that we live truly, deal truly, and speak truly. And if we make a mistake, remember: "He is also able to save to the uttermost those who come to God through Him, since He always lives to make intercession for them" (Hebrews 7:25 NKJV). Receive forgiveness, get up, and keep going.

This call goes forth to the Church of the Living God for unity. Unity assures the Church of answered prayer—of victory. Jesus prays we would be one even as He and the Father are one. In the book of Ephesians, Paul writes about the glorious Church. This is the Church united. Out of chaos shall come forth order and unity; each member of the Body of Christ taking his place, submitted to God and by His grace we stand for truth and righteousness. We believe and proclaim: *there is one Lord and one Body!*

Hear therefore, O Israel, and observe to do *it;* that it may be well with thee, and that ye may increase mightily, as the LORD God of thy fathers hath promised thee, in the land that floweth with milk and honey. *Hear, O Israel: The LORD our God is one LORD:* And thou shalt love the LORD thy God with all thine heart, and with all thy soul, and with all thy might.

Deuteronomy 6:3-5

This prayer is written to pray over a nation or continent you feel strongly about. It may be your own nation or another. Take a moment to pray God's Word over that land:

PRAYERS THAT AVAIL MUCH®
NATIONS AND CONTINENTS

Father, Jesus is our Salvation. He is the God-revealing light to the non-Jewish nations and the light of glory for Your people Israel. As members of the Body of Christ, we are asking You to give us the nations for an inheritance and the ends of the earth for our possession. All kings shall fall down before You; all nations shall serve You. In the name of Jesus, we bring before You the nation (or continent) of _____ and her leaders. We ask You to rebuke ungodly leaders for our sakes, so that we may live a quiet and peaceable life in all godliness and honesty.

We pray that skillful and godly wisdom will enter the heart of _____'s leaders and that knowledge shall be pleasant to them, that discretion will watch over them, and that understanding will keep them and deliver them from the way of evil and from evil men.

We pray and believe that the good news of the Gospel is published in this land. We thank You for laborers of the harvest to publish Your Word that Jesus is Lord in _____. We thank You for raising up intercessors to pray for _____in Jesus' name. Amen.

SCRIPTURE REFERENCES

1 Timothy 2:1,2; Proverbs 2:10-15 AMP; Psalm 68:11; Luke 10:2

ANSWER THE CALL

1. When Jesus prayed for the Church in John 17, what was He most concerned about?_____

_____

2. In Mark 11, Jesus displayed great anger when He overturned the money changers' tables. What was He upset about?_____

_____

_____

3. In Luke 11, what did the disciples want to know from Jesus? Why?_____

_____

4. Why do believers seem to struggle to get along? What can you do to change it?_____

_____

CHAPTER 2
WHO IS CALLED TO PRAY?

Pray at all times (on every occasion, in every season) in the Spirit, with all [manner of] prayer and entreaty. To that end keep alert and watch with strong purpose *and* perseverance, interceding in behalf of all the saints (God's consecrated people).

Ephesians 6:18 AMP

S everal years ago after a number of strenuous days of ministering and taking care of my home, four children, and my husband, I walked out of a difficult meeting where I had been speaking. I complained loud and long about what I believed to be the root cause of the problem—my intercessors were obviously not doing their job. Had they been, I reasoned, my teaching and ministry would be going much more smoothly.

When I finally settled down long enough to quit murmuring and complaining, the Lord revealed something to me about prayer. It was during football season, and He used a football game (of all things) to show me how He holds each person responsible for his own personal prayer life.

My husband was at work, the children snug in their beds, and I decided to watch a football game to gain better understanding of the sport. At least I knew the difference between the defensive and offensive lines. As the gigantic men lined up glaring at each other I saw this as no ordinary ballgame, but a line of intercessors, people taking a stand against the opponents, ready to charge the powers of darkness. One or two others were dashing around while a ball was hiked by someone who was calling the plays. Suddenly, this was no quarterback, but a minister directing and calling the plays that were taking place. I knew if anyone on the team was out of position or failed to do his job, his actions would affect all the other team members.

That's when it hit me like a ton of bricks: no matter how well the linemen (intercessors) and others played their positions, they needed their leader. Without the well-prepared, mentally alert, physically able-bodied quarterback, winning was virtually an impossible task. I also realized the quarterback could not lead his team to victory without the proper preparation and willingness to accept and follow the instructions of his coach.

Once that analogy became clear to me, it didn't take me more than a few seconds to see I had been wrong in my attitude and actions. I realized I needed to repent of having laid the blame for my failure on my "teammates." The real fault was mine for having neglected my responsibility to spend time conferring directly with my "Divine Coach" and carefully following His game plan. We all have a part in God's divine game plan. The Message Bible makes this so clear in the book of Ephesians:

> This is no afternoon athletic contest that we'll walk away from and forget about in a couple of hours. This is for keeps, a life-or-death fight to the finish against the Devil and all his angels. Be prepared. You're up against far more than you can handle on your own. Take all the help you can get, every weapon God has issued, so that when it's all over but the shouting you'll still be on your feet.
>
> Ephesians 6:12-13 MSG

The entire Body of Christ, working together in harmony with the Holy Spirit and each other, will produce positive results. Every member of the Body has a place in the Church. Our foundation is the Word of God; our standard, the banner of love; our clothing, humility.

WE ARE ALL CALLED TO PRAY

As I have grown into a level of spiritual understanding concerning prayer, I've realized it is a privilege and honor to be a co-laborer with God. Individually, we are parts of one another—mutually dependent upon one another. Jesus did not single out certain individuals to pray. In Luke 18:1 AMP, He indicated to us collectively that we, "ought always to pray and not to turn coward (faint, lose heart, and give up)." In 1 Timothy 2:1 Paul says everyone is to pray—offering petitions, prayers, intercessions, and thanksgiving on behalf of all men. Jesus says for us to watch and pray so that we will not enter into temptation. (Matthew 26:41.) That injunction includes everybody!

Ideally, ministers maintain an effective prayer life, keeping their fellowship with God current. They are surrounded by diverse members of the Body of Christ who have answered the call to pray. If you are in a position of ministry, it is especially important for you to spend consistent time in prayer.

Pastor Lane Holland, co-author of *Prayers That Avail Much®* *for Leaders*, wrote: "Several years ago I heard an interview with a pastor who was well seasoned in both years and pastoral ministry. When asked how he kept up with all the responsibilities of ministering to his large congregation and spending quality time with his family, he responded by holding up his rather well-worn Bible. His answer to the host was that the more his responsibilities increased, the more time he spent in personal prayer and study of the Word. He said it would have been impossible to consistently have a fresh word for his congregation, enjoy his family, and have the spiritual stamina to sustain himself through the years without having learned to listen for the voice of his Master." [1]

JESUS IS OUR EXAMPLE

We may study the lives of many successful people in the ministry, but it is Jesus who is our most effective role model for leadership. It is amazing how often we have read the New Testament, seeing the miraculous public ministry of our Lord, but failing to recognize the key to His success. Jesus was a person of prayer; He spent much time fellowshipping with the Father. He spoke what He heard the Father say, and He did what He saw the Father do. Most of those times of prayer and communion were spent in solitude—apart even from His intimate friends and disciples.

In Luke 11:1 we see Jesus' disciples come to Him and ask Him to teach them to pray. Obviously they recognized the source of His power emanated from His Father through prayer. Too often our prayer time is controlled by our needs—usually, our desperate needs. Crises, however, never dictated the prayer life of Jesus. He prayed before His times of public ministry and afterwards. The results were evident.

We ourselves have heard and seen, "How God anointed and consecrated Jesus of Nazareth with the [Holy] Spirit and with strength and ability and power; how He went about doing good and, in particular, curing all who were harassed and oppressed by [the power of] the devil, for God was with Him" (Acts 10:38 AMP). Yet the amazing thing is, Jesus tells His followers: "I assure you, most solemnly I tell you, if any one steadfastly believes in Me, he will himself be able to do the things I do; and he will do even greater things than these, because I go to the Father" (John 14:12 AMP). Then why are we not yet regularly and systematically producing these "greater works?" Could the answer be a failure to pray? If so, we are not alone in this fault.

When Jesus prays, the heavens are open and the will of God is revealed in every situation as the natural is changed into the supernatural and the Father is glorified. In His hour of greatest need, however, Jesus calls three of His closest disciples to accompany Him, requesting they stay awake and pray. They fail Him—just as we often do. (Matthew 26:36-40.) After Jesus is resurrected, however, the disciples give themselves to study of the Word and prayer. (Acts 6:4.) We may feel as if we have failed at times, but don't let that be an excuse to stop praying. Just as the disciples made a decision to pray consistently, we can do the same. If we miss our prayer time for a day or a week or whatever the case may be, we can start again.

Today, we stand in a pivotal point in history. Never has intercession been more necessary than now. Rather than blaming others for the condition of the world, let's remember we are not in a "flesh and blood struggle," but a battle against the spiritual powers of darkness—a battle we win in prayer. (Ephesians 6:12) The time has come for the entire Church to answer the call to prayer. Let us set aside our differences that cause divisions, and come together in harmony and agreement, which will come about as we pray scripturally, led by the Spirit. Our cry must be: Your Kingdom come, Your will be done on earth as it is in heaven![2]

PAUL INSTRUCTS US TO PRAY

In the church at Philippi, there was an occasion for a church to split because two women in positions of leadership were of differing opinions. Paul instructs the church to, "...help these [two women to keep on cooperating]" (Philippians 4:3 AMP). Paul points out that they had toiled along with him in the spreading of the Gospel. We can see the attitude in which Paul prays, and how he prays by examining Philippians 1:4 AMP: "In every prayer of mine I always make my entreaty and petition for you all with joy (delight)."

As you continue to read the book of Philippians, you will see prayers Paul prays for the members while under the inspiration of the Holy Spirit. Here we have an example set before us by one who said, "Follow my example, as I follow the example of Christ" (1 Corinthians 11:1 NIV). Paul, the Apostle, prays for the churches!

We also find in Ephesians 6:18-20 AMP, Paul admonishes the church at Ephesus to pray:

Pray at all times (on every occasion, in every season) in the Spirit, with all [manner of] prayer and entreaty. To that end keep alert and watch with strong purpose and perseverance, interceding in behalf of all the saints (God's consecrated people).

And [pray] also for me, that [freedom of] utterance may be given me, that I may open my mouth to proclaim boldly the mystery of the good news (the Gospel),

For which I am an ambassador in a coupling chain [in prison. Pray] that I may declare it boldly and courageously, as I ought to do.

The Body of Christ is called to a life of prayer. Each of us is responsible to adjust our opinions and make a decision to come into the unity of the Spirit and faith by praying according to the Word of God in the Spirit. In Matthew 21:13 AMP Jesus noted, "The Scripture says, My house shall be called a house of prayer."

Individually, each of us is a temple of the Holy Spirit, or a house of prayer. The many individuals, or houses, make up one great household of prayer. Paul sets forth this concept beautifully in Ephesians 2:20-22 AMP:

You are built upon the foundation of the apostles and prophets with Christ Jesus Himself the chief Cornerstone.

In Him the whole structure is joined (bound, welded) together harmoniously, and it continues to rise (grow, increase) into a holy temple in the Lord [a sanctuary dedicated, consecrated, and sacred to the presence of the Lord].

In Him [and in fellowship with one another] you yourselves also are being built up [into this structure] with the rest, to form a fixed abode (dwelling place) of God in (by, through) the Spirit.

Let each member of the Body of Christ put on the full armor of God and actively stand against the forces of darkness. When each one of us assumes his or her position on the team or in the army of intercessors, miracles will begin to take place...the plan of God for today will start to unfold. We will become one in Christ Jesus so the world will know that God the Father has sent His Son for their salvation:

For because of Him the whole body (the church, in all its various parts), closely joined and firmly knit together by the joints and ligaments with which it is supplied, when each part [with power adapted to its need] is working properly [in all its functions], grows to full maturity, building itself up in love.

Ephesians 4:16 AMP

As we become more enlightened we assume our God-appointed task in prayer, giving place to and esteeming our supporting team members.

Join me in this prayer for unity:

PRAYERS THAT AVAIL MUCH®
UNITY AND HARMONY

Father, in the name of Jesus, this is the confidence that we have in You: that, if we ask anything according to Your will, You hear us; and since we know that You hear us, whatsoever we ask, we know that we have the petitions that we desire of You.

Holy Spirit, teach us how to agree (harmonize together, together make a symphony)—about anything and everything—so that whatever we ask will come to pass and be done for us by our Father in heaven.

We pray that as members of the Body of Christ we will live as becomes us—with complete lowliness of mind (humility) and meekness (unselfishness, gentleness, mildness), with patience, bearing with one another and making allowances because we love one another. In the name of Jesus, we are eager and strive earnestly to guard and keep the harmony and oneness of [produced by] the Spirit in the binding power of peace.

Father, thank You that Jesus has given to us the glory and honor that You gave Him, that we may be one, [even] as You and Jesus are one: Jesus in us and You in Jesus, in order that we may become one and perfectly united, that the world may know and [definitely] recognize that You sent Jesus and that You have loved them [even] as You have loved Jesus. Amen.

SCRIPTURE REFERENCES

1 John 5: 14-15; 1 Corinthians 1:10 AMP; Matthew 18:19 AMP; Ephesians 4:2-3 AMP; 1 Peter 3:8-9 AMP; John 17:22-23; Matthew 6:10

ANSWER THE CALL

1.   Who does the Bible say is called to pray? (Luke 18:1; 1 Timothy 2:1)_____

_____

_____

2.   What did God anoint Jesus to do according to Acts 10:38?

_____

_____

3.   In John 14:12 what does Jesus tell us we can do?_____

_____

_____

4.   How often does Paul instruct the Christians to pray in Ephesians 6:18-20?_____

_____

_____

5.   Is it possible to pray at all times and in all seasons?___

_____

_____

CHAPTER 3
CONDITIONS FOR ANSWERED PRAYER

And how bold and free we then become in his presence, freely asking according to his will, sure that he's listening. And if we're confident that he's listening, we know that what we've asked for is as good as ours.

1 John 5:14-15 MSG

Everyone who prays desires their prayers be answered, but some fail to pray because they do not know the power of prayer or they have experienced disappointment in their past prayer life. Yet, often even the most distant unbeliever will call out to God in crisis. Something inside all of us knows to pray.

God does hear our prayers. But you may wonder why some prayers are answered and some seem to be unanswered. The Father, in His Word, has given us spiritual laws that govern prayer. They do not represent bondage, but the freedom to approach the Throne of Grace with confidence and faith. Obedience to these laws originates with love and confidence in the One who had men of the Bible to write about prayer. Obedience to these principles brings amazing answers to prayer.

The Bible is a loving revelation of who God is and who we are. He gave His children rights and privileges through His Son, Christ Jesus, preparing the way to a more intimate relationship with the Triune God. Your particular need is covered in this great Book of the ages. Study what the Bible says about your situation until you are fully persuaded God will answer your petitions you present to Him with thanksgiving. He said He would supply your every need.[1]

Discovering a Prayer Relationship

Although I accepted Jesus as my Savior at the age of twelve, in January 1969, I sat at my kitchen table contemplating suicide—having convinced myself that my husband and four children would be better off without me. To my utter astonishment, a great Light came into the room. Radiant beams focused on the very spot where I sat. When I looked up, the yellow walls seemed to vibrate with life and everything appeared new. The world inside and outside was bathed in purity and I sat mesmerized, wondering what was happening.

My kitchen disappeared and in its place a field of hardened, brown, crusty, fallow ground stretched out under a blue sky. Gazing upon the landscape I saw a man at the far corner plowing the unbroken field and beneath the stiff, dry ground was moist, fertile soil. A dam broke within me and I began to sob almost violently as furrow after furrow was plowed.

Memories and emotions from countless hurts and disappointments rushed past me. I heard a voice saying, "Old things are passed away; behold, all things are become new" (2 Corinthians 5:17). I didn't know, but the Lord was preparing my heart for the planting of His Word, just as He says in Mark 4:20: "And these are they which are sown on good ground; such as hear the word, and receive it, and bring forth fruit, some thirtyfold, some sixty, and some an hundred."

When this vision was completed, I had an insatiable desire to read the Bible, and I read it as though God had written this sixty-six volume Book directly to me.

The Person I had thought of as an "All Seeing Eye" peering at my every mistake became the Father who was watching over me and my family with eyes of love and a heart of compassion.

Knowing God became my motivation for living and reading the Bible was my lifeline to Him…the Triune Being. I devoured chapters and chapters of God's Word every day, and His Word became my prayer style, although I didn't call it "prayer." The depression, fears, and insecurities began to give way to glorious, joyous fellowship with the Triune Being; Father, Son, and Holy Spirit. This was the beginning of my prayer life. Each moment of every day He walked with me and He talked with me.

THE BEGINNING OF PRAYERS THAT AVAIL MUCH®

A few years later I began teaching Bible studies and establishing prayer groups when the unthinkable occurred. In his junior year of high school, our son became a stranger to us. We talked with teachers, counselors, psychologists, and psychiatrists only to discover there was no human solution to his drug addiction. With my Bible, pen, and paper ready, I asked the Holy Spirit to teach me to pray. I cried, listened to teaching tapes, and made notes from my Bible and a book on prayer, *In His Presence*, by E. W. Kenyon—a book that had been recommended to me by my dad, Rev. A. H. "Buck" Griffin.

Our son's need for deliverance began my introduction to spiritual warfare, which I didn't understand at the time. As I studied I was surprised to learn this warfare was taking place in the battlefield of my mind. The judgmental, critical attitude I had held was challenged by the love of God. Jesus' attitude toward sinners, the story of the prodigal son, and the account of Jesus' actions concerning Peter created havoc with my sense of justice. When Jesus knew Satan was going to test Peter, He didn't rebuke the devil or stop him. Instead, he prayed Peter's faith would not fail. (Luke 22:31-32.) Jesus didn't reprimand Peter, but told him that after he was converted he was to strengthen his brethren.

Asking myself what would Jesus do about the situation with our son left me in a puzzled state of mind. How were we to discipline our son or punish him so he would turn from his evil ways? Isaiah 54:13 became my mantra for David, "And all thy children shall be taught of the LORD; and great shall be the peace of thy children," but it would be a few years before I really heard that only God Himself would be David's teacher. As I grew in the grace and knowledge of Jesus Christ, I became more willing to let go and let God. The day came when I did completely let go!

Much of my praying was dictated by circumstances, my shame, and soulish desires. Over the years the Holy Spirit taught me the difference between spiritual warfare, intercession, and other kinds of prayer. Along the way, my prayer life went through a metamorphosis. I learned about *all manner* of prayer.[2] I quit *fighting* the devil, and learned instead to resist his wiles and stand according to the sixth chapter of Ephesians.

By the inspiration of the Holy Spirit, I began building up the hedge and standing in the gap[3] before the Father, which is intercession. I learned about the power of praise, and about the correlation between grace and supplication, which is asking for mercy. (Many times in my anger, I would have withheld mercy from our son, *but God!*)

You will read more about the kinds of prayer later in this book and the Holy Spirit will teach you if you ask Him. For many years my prayers flowed like rivers of living water. I wrote and enlisted prayer group members to write powerful Scriptural prayers that later became a bestselling book known as *Prayers That Avail Much*®. Due to prayer requests, other volumes were added.

THE POWER OF SCRIPTURAL PRAYER

Praying Scriptural prayers helps you renew your mind to what God says about you and your situation, and you will find it easier to resist the temptation to be squeezed into the conceptual mold of this present evil world. The Word of God is powerful especially when spoken over your life. The Holy Spirit helps you rid yourself of wrong motives and attitudes, that you might establish God's will to meet your need. His Word gives you the ability to take your thoughts captive and bring them into subjection to God's Word. Do not entertain fear or engage in rigidity, denial, or emotional isolation. The promised land of rest and peace belonged to the children of Israel, but they "could not enter in because of unbelief" (Hebrews 3:19). The Apostle Peter explains God's rest in the opening of his second book:

> May grace (God's favor) and peace (which is perfect well-being, all necessary good, all spiritual prosperity, and freedom from fears and agitating passions and moral conflicts) will be multiplied to you in [the full, personal, precise, and correct] knowledge of God and of Jesus our Lord.
>
> 2 Peter 1:2 AMP

Settle in your mind and heart that it is God's will to meet your need. It may take time to overcome thoughts and feelings of fear, but the end result is amazing! Purpose to become single-minded on God's Word and know there is nothing that can stop His Word from being written on the tablets of your heart and mind.

After you have prayed according to the will and purpose of God, you can then use spiritual weapons to cast down every imagination, theory, religious precept, philosophy and reasoning which sets itself against the knowledge of God found in His Word. (2 Corinthians 10:5.) Most people have formed patterns of thinking that are contrary to the ways of God. It is your responsibility to bring every thought into captivity, destroying every psychological stronghold with the Gospel of Christ, establishing a new fortress for Kingdom living. This means casting aside worry and anxiety about the outcome of that for which you have prayed. (1 Peter 5:7; Philippians 4:6.) Only through a healthy relationship with the Father God will you see this come to fulfillment in your life. Don't try to reduce God to your idea of Him, but allow the Word to shape who God is and wants to be in your life.

Refuse to see past mistakes as failures; consider them as stepping-stones which will take you from glory to glory by the Holy Spirit. Circumstances are created through the decision-making process. The Holy Spirit will guide your decisions; however the results of your choices sometimes conflict with spiritual laws already in motion.

You may be in a desperate situation even as you read this book and I encourage you to look to God for deliverance. Believe God has already delivered you from all your destructions and He will show you the way out. (Psalm 107:20.) Through the eye of faith, look at things that are not seen rather than things that are seen[4]; what you can see is temporal and subject to change by the Word of God.

Abraham, the father of faith, praised God for the blessing even before it was physically manifested. (Romans 4:20.) Praise God for the answer, exercise patience; wait for the answer to your prayer in peace and confidence. (Hebrews 10:35, 37.)

FORGIVENESS—A KEY TO
ANSWERED PRAYER

Jesus says, "I tell you, you can pray for anything, and if you believe that you've received it, it will be yours. But when you are praying, first forgive anyone you are holding a grudge against, so that your Father in heaven will forgive your sins, too" (Mark 11:24-25 NLT). Understanding the process of true forgiveness paves the way for answered prayer. When someone has wronged you, be honest with yourself; express your true feelings and deal truly. Allow the anointing that is upon Jesus to bind up and heal your brokenness. Receive your healing which will enable you to pull down the wall of emotional isolation permitting others back into your heart. Forgiveness does not always dissipate a memory, but it does eradicate the sting.

An intercessor's prayer life is dependent on God's grace. A sincere desire to have a successful prayer life necessitates looking beyond situations, problems, and circumstances. Forgive and praise the God of all creation, worship Him in spirit and truth. Call the things which be not as though they were just as Abraham did as our example in Romans 4:16-22:

Therefore it is of faith, that it might be by grace; to the end the promise might be sure to all the seed; not to that only which is of the law, but to that also which is of the faith of Abraham; who is the father of us all,

(As it is written, I have made thee a father of many nations,) before him whom he believed, even God, who quickeneth the dead, and calleth those things which be not as though they were. Who against hope believed in hope, that he might become the father of many nations, according to that which was spoken, So shall thy seed be.

And being not weak in faith, he considered not his own body now dead, when he was about an hundred years old, neither yet the deadness of Sarah's womb: He staggered not at the promise of God through unbelief; but was strong in faith, giving glory to God; And being fully persuaded that, what he had promised, he was able also to perform. And therefore it was imputed to him for righteousness.

Hebrews 10: 35-36 NKJV also gives us great encouragement to have patience: "Do not cast away your confidence, which has great reward. For you have need of endurance, so that after you have done the will of God, you may receive the promise."

ABIDE IN CHRIST

Jesus reveals the all-inclusive condition of answered prayer in His message to His disciples on the way to the Garden of

Gethsemane: "If ye abide in me, and my words abide in you, ye shall ask what ye will, and it shall be done unto you" (John 15:7). This is an amazing promise that Jesus so boldly makes to us. He gives us this promise, and also prays for us, "That they all may be one; as thou, Father, art in me, and I in thee, that they also may be one in us" (John 17:21).

This is the key to answered prayer: abiding in Him—the true Vine. Psalm 91:1 AMP says it this way: "He Who dwells in the secret place of the Most High shall remain stable and fixed under the shadow of the Almighty [Whose power no foe can withstand]."

After you have done all to stand, you will be able to stand until the answer is apparent to all. Jesus states He is the Vine and we are the branches. (John 15:5.) A branch standing alone cannot bear fruit, but receives its life from the vine. Our Lord promises if we would abide in Him, we would produce fruit—prayer fruit. The fruit of the Spirit is listed in Galatians, chapter 5; here Jesus is speaking of prayer fruit. It is an absolute prerequisite we abide in the Vine and bear fruit, knowing without Him we can do nothing.

Many have overlooked one statement Jesus made in this chapter. He says if we do not abide in Him we will be cut off. (John 15:6.) Prayer is essential to the eternal welfare of each individual believer. Man has been created for God's pleasure and to bring glory to Him: "Herein is my Father glorified, that ye bear much fruit; so shall ye be my disciples" (John 15:8).

Jesus says He came to finish the work of the Father. (John 4:34.) Work while it is yet day for the night is coming when no man can work. (John 9:4.) Follow the example of Jesus and finish the work that remains—bearing prayer fruit, preparing the way of the Lord. Be available not only to pray, but also to serve as the Father leads you in any area of ministry. It is in giving of yourself that you will find joy. A fruit-bearing intercessor is a joyful intercessor.

After Jesus reveals the conditions of answered prayer, He declares the blessings of abiding in Him. One of those blessings is to rejoice with joy unspeakable and full of glory. (1 Peter 1:8.) The Message Bible says with singing and laughter.

The first prerequisite is that we dwell in God's love by obeying His commandment to love one another. (John 15:12-15.) We are to keep the commandment just as Jesus did. He assures us that if we abide in the Vine, producing prayer fruit and obeying the Father, His joy will remain in us and our joy will be full. (John 16:24.)

SOWING AND REAPING

The law of sowing and reaping works in the prayer arena. There is a time to sow and a time to reap. "[Remember] this:

he who sows sparingly and grudgingly will also reap sparingly and grudgingly, and he who sows generously [that blessings may come to someone] will also reap generously and with blessings" (2 Corinthians 9:6 AMP).

Don't wait for problems to force you to pray. Be ready for prayer assignments from the Holy Spirit. "Devote yourselves to prayer with an alert mind and a thankful heart" (Colossians 4:2 NLT). It is in the good times seed is sown; then when the harvest comes, you will be ready to reap. When you sow in prayer, God will put you into someone's prayers and you will reap the benefits of someone else's intercession. Start sowing today, so a season of reaping begins as well.

"The liberal person shall be enriched, and he who waters shall himself be watered" (Proverbs 11:25 AMP). Water is a symbol of the Holy Spirit, and as you pray, water will flow out into the desert, into the lives of others.

Again I use my mother as a modern day example. Several years ago she was attacked with a physical illness that threatened to take away her joy and diminish her prayer time. In spite of the pain in her body, early morning found her worshiping her heavenly Father and interceding for others, as rivers of living water flowed from within her innermost being. As a result, any time she needed to drink from the living water, it was there for her.

The week my mother's problem began, a pastor's wife called me to ask about my mother. She related how an image of Donnis kept coming before her in prayer. She stated she had no idea why God called her to the place of prayer on my mother's behalf, and wanted to know if there was any prayer need I knew about.

The pain was almost more than Donnis could bear, but through the intercession of one who obeyed the call to prayer she maintained "the good fight of faith" (1 Timothy 6:12). During the first week of this trial, she concealed her pain from those in her household, going right on about her normal activities—cooking meals, taking a neighbor to the hospital, shopping with her week-long visitor, and keeping up the solid front of joy. God began to move upon the hearts of other intercessors to pray for her.

Over the next few weeks, as family and friends heard about her need they stood with her. She never wavered in her faith, and God sent forth His Word and healed her. (Psalm 107:20.)

Sow in season, and you will reap the harvest.

SEEK FIRST THE KINGDOM OF GOD

Seek first the Kingdom of God, and His righteousness. (Matthew 6:33.) God's Kingdom is not ushered in with visible signs. (Luke 17:20.) It is a mystery. Natural man (the unsaved person) does not receive the things of the Spirit of God, for they are foolishness to him. (1 Corinthians 2:14.) However, I have good news; it has been given to the Christian to know the mystery of the Kingdom. (Mark 4:11.) This knowledge is spiritually discerned. As you seek God through reading His Word and prayer, He will reveal Himself to you.

If you are not praying for your family or your church, begin now. Pray for those who persecute you. Pray for all churches, all denominations, all nations. The more you pray, the more the Holy Spirit will expand your capacity for prayer. Become sensitive to Kingdom situations, receiving, and cultivating the true intercession of Jesus. You can start by praying the following prayer for the people of our land.

PRAYERS THAT AVAIL MUCH®
THE PEOPLE OF OUR LAND

Father, in the name of Jesus, we come before You to claim Your promise in 2 Chronicles 7:14 AMP: "If My people, who are called by My name, shall humble themselves, pray, seek, crave, and require of necessity My face and turn from their wicked ways, then I will hear from heaven, forgive their sin, and heal their land."

We are Your people, called by Your name. Thank you for hearing our prayers and moving by Your Spirit in our land. There are famines, earthquakes, floods, natural disasters, and violence occurring. Men's hearts are failing them because of fear.

Lord, Your Son, Jesus, spoke of discerning the signs of the times. With the Holy Spirit as our Helper, we are watching and praying.

We desire to humble ourselves before You, asking that a spirit of humility be released in us. Thank You for quiet and meek spirits, for we know that the meek shall inherit the earth.

Search us, O God, and know our hearts; try us, and know our thoughts for today. See if there be any wicked way in us, and lead us in the way of everlasting.

Forgive us our sins of judging inappropriately, complaining about, and criticizing our leaders. Touch our lips with coals from Your altar that we may pray prayers that avail much for all men and women everywhere.

Lord, we desire to release rivers of living water for the healing of the nations. Amen.

SCRIPTURE REFERENCES:

Luke 21:11, 25, 26; Matthew 16:3; Matthew 26:41; James 4:10; 1 Peter 3:4; Matthew 5:5; Psalm 139:23; Isaiah 6:6, 7 NIV; James 5:16; 1 Timothy 2:1; John 7:38; Revelation 22:1-2

ANSWER THE CALL:

1. Why is it so important to pray according to God's Word? (See 2 Timothy 3:16.) _____

_____

2. Is it possible to forgive someone even if you still remember what they've done? (See Mark 11:24-25.) _____

_____

3. What does it mean to you to "abide in Christ" as Jesus states in John 15:5-8? _____

_____

4. How are the things of God discerned? (See 1 Corinthians 2:14.) Have you discerned any certain thing from reading the Bible?_____

_____

CHAPTER 4
HOW TO ENTER IN

You have endowed him with eternal blessings and given
him the joy of your presence. For the king trusts in the
LORD. The unfailing love of the Most High will keep
him from stumbling.

Psalm 21:6-7 NLT

Even though I share from the Scriptures a "process" for
entering into intimacy with God, none of this matters
unless you have fallen in love with the Person, Jesus Christ.
To love Him is to love the Father. It's all about relationship—
God's love for humanity. I remember when I fell in love with
my husband I woke each morning with a sense of satisfaction,
a sense of joy because I had met someone who loved me and
accepted me and thought I was the greatest gift he had ever
received. (This love was tested and tried as the years rolled along.)

Oh, how I wish I could bring to the surface the words that swirl deep within me—words too wonderful for expression. I know they are there, words I've never written or spoken. Maybe if I were a poet I could pen a description of this love affair I have every day with the God of the universe.

There's more to it than I know how to express…I can only say it's a mystery. The day I fell in love with Jesus can't be described although I've tried to share it many times. I've wished I could package it and hold it out for the world to see. My prayer life grew out of my relationship with a Person who is the "I AM," who loves me unconditionally. He receives each one of us "just as I am without one plea…."[1]

The Holy Spirit taught me and led me to pray for others. The Scriptures teach God creates each of us by Christ Jesus to join him in the work He does, the good work He has prepared for us to do. (Ephesians 2:10.) He created a desire in me to pray for others, and it was not burdensome because I was in love with the Triune Being…a Person…the great Three in One. My joy knew no bounds.

In Philippians 1:4 AMP, the Apostle Paul writes: "In every prayer of mine I always make my entreaty and petition for you all with joy (delight)." You do not have to be so overwhelmed by the needs of others that you neglect your fellowship with God. In fact, in the long run diving into intercession without fellowship day after day will greatly hinder you and drain you of strength. The Father has invited you to be in true communion with Him each and every day. There may be days He only wants you to fellowship with Him, praise and worship Him in spirit and in truth. At those times you rest from your prayer labor.

Moses was an intercessor who knew how to enter into this communication with God. The Lord promised His presence would go with Moses and He would give him rest. Moses knew the key to experiencing this rest was spending time alone with God. In order for you to prepare for intercession you will find it necessary to do as Moses did. Make time every day for communion with your Father—spirit to Spirit.

Psalm 100 gives an outline (or formula for those who like steps one, two, and three) for entering into a specified prayer time or time of devotion, which is where true intercession begins.

First, Make a Joyful Noise to the Lord

First, "Make a joyful noise to the Lord" (Psalm 100:1 AMP). Do this regardless of circumstances. Say: "This is the day which the LORD has made; I will rejoice and be glad in it" (Psalm 118:24).

Second, Serve the Lord with Gladness

Second, "Serve the Lord with gladness! Come before His presence with singing!" (Psalm 100:2 AMP). Begin your prayer time by delighting yourself in the Lord, for happy is the person whose God is the Lord. (Psalm 144:15.) He desires you serve Him with gladness of heart. He supplies fountains of joy within you—He has made you glad! (Psalm 92:4.) Come into His presence with singing, for He has put a new song in your heart. Release it in words and music, "Speak out...in psalms and hymns and spiritual songs... making melody with all your heart to the Lord" (Ephesians 5:19 AMP). Dance before Him, putting off burdens and heavy loads. Make a joyful noise to the Lord!

THIRD, KNOW THE LORD IS GOD

Third, "Know (perceive, recognize, and understand with approval) that the Lord is God! It is He Who has made us, not we ourselves [and we are His]! We are His people and the sheep of His pasture" (Psalm 100:3 AMP). Exalt the Lord your God. (Psalm 99:5.) Eulogize Him! The Word is God, and in order to know Him, you must become acquainted with Him through His Word (the Bible) and the Holy Spirit (our Teacher).

Today, so often the work of the enemy is attributed to God by people who have not taken the time to get acquainted with "Our Father which art in heaven." They are unable to "hallow" His Name because they do not know Him.[2]

In order to pray effectively, learn who God is. The many different names of God in the Old Testament reveal His nature and character and it's all good. We do not dictate our will to God, but rather we remember He is the Maker, the Creator, and the Potter. He has our best in store for us. "We are His people, and the sheep of His pasture" (Psalm 100:3).

Discover Who You are in Christ

Do you know the kind of person you are? Through the positive confession of God's Word, you can begin to see yourself as God sees you. The Holy Spirit will help you identify your strengths and your weaknesses. Sometimes we are our own worst enemy. We become deceived in areas in which we merely listen to the Word of God, but never obey it. Always be willing to apply the Word to daily living. Believe what God says about you in His Word. Always be ready to submit to the constant ministry of transformation by the Holy Spirit.

It is imperative, for instance, that you know you are God's handiwork, recreated in Christ Jesus: you are His very own workmanship.[3] As you pray, the Holy Spirit will enable you to see yourself and others as God sees His people—the sheep of His pasture. In Romans 8:37 Paul says we are "more than conquerors through him that loved us." This perspective will build confidence toward the God who answers prayer and faith in His ability within you to pray effectively.

After my first visit to Israel I understood even more about being His sheep, walking through the valley of the shadow of death, about

His rod and staff that comfort me.[4] I'm thankful I'm a sheep of His pasture. I'm thankful to be dependent upon Him and not my own natural ability. When things seem beyond my control, He is there to calm me down and bring me through the storms of life.

This, then, is the third step to entering into intercessory prayer—to declare who God is, and who He created you to be.

FOURTH, ENTER INTO HIS GATES WITH THANKSGIVING

Fourth, "Enter into His gates with thanksgiving and a thank offering and into His courts with praise! Be thankful and say so to Him, bless and affectionately praise His name!" (Psalm 100:4 AMP). Be grateful to the Lord for what He has done and for the things He has given you. Do not come to the place where you take God and His works for granted. Reiterate His wondrous works and mighty deeds in your life and in the lives of those for whom you intercede. Be thankful for the family God has given you. You may or may not feel thankful for them at the time! But as you pray for your family, God is able to move in their life. Perhaps you do not have a large family, but God will give you a family of friends in your church. Rejoice in the gifts He gives you as friends.

You are responsible for praying for the members of your family. God is looking for an intercessor in each family who will love as Jesus loves, laying down his (or her) life for family members and loved ones.

My mother was the first one in her family to receive Jesus as her Lord and Savior. As a fifteen year-old, she paved the way for her entire family (including her parents) to come to the knowledge of the truth. Later she and my dad were married. As we children were born my mother began to pray diligently for us. Until she went to be with the Lord at the age of 81 her daily prayers included not only her children, but also their spouses, grandchildren, and great-grandchildren. Today, her prayer mantle has passed down to others. She declared on the authority of God's Word all her posterity belongs to the Kingdom of God and her prayers are in the throne room of heaven for eternity.

When you answer the call to pray, assume the responsibility of praying for your family, pray for those in leadership, and answer the call to pray for the nations. I've had mothers to declare they will "worry" about their children until they die because they love them. "Worry" and "love" are not synonymous. In Philippians 4:6 AMP, Paul urges: "Do not fret or have any anxiety about anything, but in every circumstance and in everything, by prayer and petition (definite requests), with thanksgiving, continue to make your wants known to God."

FIFTH, FOR THE LORD IS GOOD

Fifth, "For the Lord is good; His mercy and loving-kindness are everlasting, His faithfulness and truth endure to all generations" (Psalm 100:5 AMP). Remember this truth and rejoice in it. Don't get so caught up in family iniquities and curses that you forget the family blessings! God is greater than all our sin and the sins of our forefathers.

Those who pray for others are not to be of a sad countenance, burdened, or heavy laden. Happy are we whose God is the Lord.[5] Most intercessors I know have a good sense of humor, and they are quick to laugh. If you are feeling overburdened run to Jesus who said:

Come to Me, all you who labor and are heavy-laden and over burdened, and I will cause you to rest.[I will ease and relieve and refresh your souls.]

Take my yoke upon you and learn of Me, for I am gentle (meek) and humble (lowly) in heart, and you will find rest (relief and ease and refreshment and recreation and blessed quiet) for your souls.

For My yoke is wholesome (useful, good—not harsh, hard, sharp, or pressing, but comfortable, gracious, and pleasant), and My burden is light and easy to be borne.

Matthew 11:28-30 AMP

In His presence you are relieved of heavy burdens and set free to become a co-laborer together with God. Take His burden—it is light and His yoke is easy: "In Your presence is fullness of joy, at Your right hand there are pleasures forevermore" (Psalm 16:11 AMP). The Holy Spirit will show you the pathway to a life of prayer.

LEARNING TO KNOW HIS HEART, HIS VOICE

By entering into a time of praise and worship, using Psalm 100 as a model, each person has the opportunity to lay aside thoughts which interfere with, "being in full accord and of one harmonious mind and intention" (Philippians 2:2 AMP). You have the mind of Christ and hold the thoughts, feelings and purposes of His heart. (1 Corinthians 2:16.) In His presence it is easy to: "Let this same attitude and purpose and [humble] mind be in you which was in Christ Jesus" (Philippians 2:5 AMP). His purpose is stated in Luke 4:18-19 AMP:

The Spirit of the Lord [is] upon Me, because He has anointed Me [the Anointed One, the Messiah] to preach the good news (the Gospel) to the poor; He has sent Me to announce release to the captives and recovery of sight to the blind, to send forth as delivered those who are oppressed [who are downtrodden, bruised, crushed, and broken down by calamity],

To proclaim the accepted and acceptable year of the Lord[the day when salvation and the free favors of God profusely abound.]

Join with the Lord in His purpose when you pray for the poor, those in captivity, the blind, and the oppressed who are downtrodden, bruised, crushed, and broken by calamity. Through intercessory prayer, you pave the way for their salvation and the free favors of God.

Begin to pray for others as the Holy Spirit leads, remembering that He does not lead apart from the Word of God. Learn to hear His voice. Jesus says, "I am the good shepherd, and know my sheep, and am known of mine" (John 10:14). Earlier in this chapter Jesus lets us know that as His sheep, "A stranger will they not follow, but will flee from him: for they know not the voice of strangers" (John 10:5).

There are many voices, many languages. Paul says none of them is without significance. (1 Corinthians 14:10.) Some individuals say God has never spoken to them, but He has—through the pages of sixty-six books that are bound into two volumes: the Old Testament and the New Testament. God's Word will endure forever. When you know His Word, you learn to hear His voice speaking to your heart and mind. So often we dismiss a thought that comes to us without even being aware it was the Father speaking to us. I remember a song from my childhood, *"I'll Be Somewhere Listening for My Name"* by Bill Anderson.[6] The verse says, "When my Savior calls I will answer." We want to be so in tune with the Lord we don't miss His voice when He calls. That kind of intimacy comes only from spending time reading and knowing His Word.

Know God, know His Word, and pray according to His will. Locate your faith that is the faith of the Son of God. When you find God's will on a subject, mix faith with what you "hear" or understand from the written Word. Pray with conviction because you believe God.

CHECK YOUR MOTIVES

I want to give you an important principle regarding God's Word: never add to God's will by reading into the Scriptures something they do not say. For instance, you cannot take Psalm 37:4 AMP, "Delight yourself also in the Lord, and He will give you the desires and secret petitions of your heart," and use it as a basis for asking God for another person's mate, house, or car. That would be adding to God's stated will. This manner of praying will produce disastrous results, hurting many people, rather than bringing glory to the Father.

Who shall approach God? He who has clean hands and a pure heart. (Psalm 24:3-4.) In James 4:2-3 AMP the apostle tells his first century readers: "...You do not have because you do not ask. [Or] you do ask [God for them] and yet fail to receive, because you ask with wrong purpose and evil, selfish motives."

It is imperative our petitions and intercessions be made out of a heart of selflessness. True intercession is rooted and grounded in *agape* love.

When you are praying God's will for someone, it is not necessary to tell that person about your intercession. (Keeping prayer matters between you and God is a guard against pride.) Remember, you cannot force anyone to obey God. For example, the husband cannot demand his wife respect and honor him; neither can the wife demand her husband love her as Christ loved the Church.[7] It is God who watches over His Word to perform it. (Jeremiah 1:12.) Your responsibility is to pray.

The Word of God says, in order to be saved: "Believe in the Lord Jesus Christ [give yourself up to Him, take yourself out of your own keeping and entrust yourself into His keeping] and you will be saved, [and this applies both to] you and your household as well" (Acts 16:31 AMP). Pray without adding anything to God's will; believe and walk in love.

One woman shared how she had prayed almost daily for three years for her alcoholic brother to be saved. She added to God's will by telling God how to perform His Word. After becoming very weary, she asked the Lord what else she could do to receive the answer to her prayers. He told her it was time for her to believe His promises! It was only a short time after she had begun to believe and have faith in God's Word that what she had been asking in prayer came to pass. She saw the salvation of God in that situation.

NEVER GIVE UP

Your prayers for your family will avail much. Never give up—but stand, and having done all, stand. (Ephesians 6:13.) It always amazes me when a prayer is answered; it's as though it had nothing to do with me, and I give glory to the Father rejoicing because I obeyed Him when I prayed in agreement with His will. It's difficult for me to understand that my prayer on earth was important in the plan of God. By His grace you are a co-laborer with God.

Never give up on your family, the church, or your nation. Jesus says in Matthew 16:18: "Upon this rock I will build my church; and the gates of hell shall not prevail against it." You can be assured your prayers will avail much when you pray according to God's will, mix faith with your prayers, and walk in love. Isaiah confirms the power of God's Word:

> For as the rain and snow come down from the heavens, and return not there again, but water the earth and make it bring forth and sprout, that it may give seed to the sower and bread to the eater,

> So shall My word be that goes forth out of My mouth; it shall not return to Me void [without producing any effect,

useless], but it shall accomplish that which I please and purpose, and it shall prosper in the thing for which I sent it.

Isaiah 55:10-11 AMP

It is my prayer that when Jesus returns, He will find you experiencing the joys of effectual intercessory prayer and will say to you, "Well done, you upright (honorable, admirable) and faithful servant! You have been faithful and trustworthy over a little; I will put you in charge of much. Enter into and share the joy (the delight, the blessedness) which your master enjoys" (Matthew 25:21 AMP).

The following prayer is a powerful and scriptural way to enter into the presence of God:

PRAYERS THAT AVAIL MUCH®
To Rejoice in the Lord

This is the day the Lord has made. I rejoice and I am glad in it! I rejoice in You always. And again I say, I rejoice. I delight myself in You, Lord. Happy am I because God is my Lord!

Father, thank You for loving me and rejoicing over me with joy. Hallelujah! I am redeemed. I come with singing, and everlasting joy is upon my head. I obtain joy and gladness, and sorrow and sighing flee away. That spirit of rejoicing, joy, and laughter is my heritage. Where the Spirit of the Lord is, there is liberty—emancipation from bondage, freedom. I walk in that liberty.

Father, I thank You that I bear much prayer fruit. I ask in Jesus' name, and I will receive, so that my joy (gladness, delight) may be full, complete, and overflowing. The joy of the Lord is my strength. Therefore, I count it all joy, all strength, when I encounter tests or trials of any sort because I am strong in You, Father.

I have the victory in the name of Jesus. Satan is under my feet. I am not moved by adverse circumstances. I have been made the righteousness of God in Christ Jesus. I dwell in the Kingdom of God and have peace and joy in the Holy Spirit! Praise the Lord! Amen.

SCRIPTURE REFERENCES:

Psalm 118:24; Philippians 4:4; Philippians 3:1; Psalm 144:15; Zephaniah 3:17; Isaiah 51:11; 2 Corinthians 3:17; John 15:7-8; John 16:23; Nehemiah 8:10; James 1:2; Ephesians 6:10; 1 John 5:4; Ephesians 1:22; 2 Corinthians 5:7; 2 Corinthians 5:21; Romans 14:17

ANSWER THE CALL

1. Psalm 100 gives us a template of how to enter into the presence of the Lord. The Scripture starts, "Make a joyful noise to the Lord" (100:1 AMP). Why would God want us to enter His presence this way? _____

_____

2. The second point is to serve the Lord with gladness (Psalm 100:2). In what ways can you serve the Lord with gladness? _____

_____

3. Next, the Scripture in Psalm 100:3 says to know the Lord is God. Part of knowing Him is to also know what He has done in you. What does God say about you in Ephesians 2:10 and how does that change how you feel about yourself? _____

_____

4. The fourth principle is to enter His presence with thanksgiving (Psalm 100:4). One of the most important things we have in our lives is our family or family of friends. As you thank the Lord for the family He has given you, in what areas can you specifically pray for them? _____

_____

5. The last principle is to know and acknowledge the Lord is good (Psalm 100:5), but there may be times when you don't feel that way. It's good to remember or even keep a list of things God has done for you. Then when those times of adversity come, go back to your list and remember how much God loves you and what good things he has done. What good thing(s) has God done for you?__

_____

_____

CHAPTER 5
PRAYER TIME:
JOY OR BONDAGE

You will show me the path of life; in Your presence is fullness of joy, at Your right hand there are pleasures forevermore.

Psalm 16:11 AMP

Seeking more knowledge about prayer, I asked a certain minister who I respected about a book on prayer that had been recommended to me. He said that in his opinion the book placed readers in bondage to prayer or at the least made them feel guilty about not praying enough. I thought a lot about his answer, and even though I bought the book, those remarks shouted so loudly it was difficult for me to understand the author's teachings. Later, I realized that a person's opinion is formed out of his own belief system and that system may be very different from my own.

Unfortunately, some teach prayer as a one-way communication system; it is presented as us talking to God and telling Him how we want it to be (the kind of house, car, the perfect children and husband/wife we want.) They say if we use the formulas of positive confession, pray a certain number of hours, and read our Bibles, God will perform what we ask. Prayer, Bible reading, and positive confession all have their place in the disciplined life of the follower of Jesus, but a relationship with God goes both ways—we talk to Him and He talks to us.

Some believers say we can have it "our way." Many in their attempts to prove their faith made demands on God to fulfill their soulish desires. I've seen people on the verge of bankruptcy trying to prove their faith. This belief system becomes like the latest fad. Believers had found a way to be acceptable, to belong, to be somebody. I remember asking someone at a convention if I had to carry a particular designer bag to fit in, and she gave me a blank stare even though one of those designer purses was swinging from her arm. I had to go to my prayer closet, asking for forgiveness for my critical attitude that was turning into cynicism. Time in my prayer closet, shut away with my Bible, pen and paper, was my lifeline to God Who loves all His children, Who is patient with all His children, constantly leading all His children to know Truth.

WHY WE PRAY

We pray because we are in love with this God who walks and talks with individuals on a personal level—the One who "knows us best and loves us most." Reading the Old Testament, I learned natural men like Abraham and Moses were not afraid to talk *with* God.

God wants us to receive His unconditional love and obey Him because we love Him. He wants us to talk with Him…not just throw words at Him and run off. He assures us that in His presence there is fullness of joy.[1] He sets us up so we can experience His amazing love and love Him in return.

It's interesting how Satan, the enemy of God, discourages people from praying. Instead of just doing it, they may fret about when to pray, how long to pray, or if they are praying correctly. The list of questions and doubts make so much noise, it becomes difficult to get down to business. Before we know it, our time is up and another day goes by and we haven't prayed. Guilt heaped upon guilt can find its way into our souls until we become acquainted with the enemy's wiles. Though he may, he doesn't have to use someone's book to make us feel insufficient and unwelcome in God's presence. The enemy has plenty of schemes to keep you out of God's presence, so keep your guard up and protect your time with your heavenly Father.

When Should We Pray?

Glorious testimonies from those who rise early in the morning to pray can make a night person feel guilty. The testimonies are very inspiring as we are told of the benefits of rising early to seek the Lord and it all makes perfect sense. Manifold Scriptures are given to support this practice and it seems everyone gets excited and makes the decision to adapt his or her lifestyle to include early-morning prayer time. I listen to young mothers berate themselves for missing their early-morning prayer time because they were up most of the night with a child. (They are harder on themselves than God would ever be.)

How early one gets up to pray can become a topic of conversation in some Christian circles. But who are they trying to impress? If the emphasis changes from *praying* to how *early* that praying is to be done, something is wrong. All the while there are people quietly going about obeying God, praying early, late, or at noon each day as the Spirit has directed without fanfare. Some are rising early, even going to their churches, and are experiencing great changes in their lives. Among these, however, there are those who have unconsciously become prideful, boasting about their achievement; while others are suffering from self-condemnation, wondering why they have not been able to conquer their sleeping habits. Satan supplies his thoughts to keep the controversy alive.

"As many as are led by the Spirit of God, they are the sons of God" (Romans 8:14). If you believe God desires you to rise early to keep your appointment with Him, by all means obey Him because of your love for Him. However, if you are struggling to meet someone else's expectations, be set free today to follow the Spirit of the Lord. Where the Spirit of the Lord is there is liberty![2]

Purpose to be led by the Spirit of God concerning both the time and the duration of your prayer sessions. God never intended for others to control your faith but intended we would be helpers of each other's joy.

How Long Should We Pray?

How long am I to pray? Jesus said to His disciples in the Garden of Gethsemane, "Are you so utterly unable to stay awake and keep watch with Me for one hour?" (Matthew 26:40 AMP). This statement has become the living Word of God to some and they are praying at least one hour each day. If you are just trying to imitate what others are doing, then your prayer time can easily become drudgery and just another work of the flesh. When we look at the Scriptures we are told to pray without ceasing.[3] That means our hearts are always open to the voice and leading of the Spirit of God.

Prayer is a spiritual discipline and habit-forming, but you and the Holy Spirit set your schedule. When others suggest a certain prayer time, check it out with your spirit and let your "yes" be yes, and your "no" be no.[4] Many who make the decision to pray one hour soon find that time increased. The more you pray, the more you desire to pray.

The committed intercessor is submitted to the leadership of the Spirit of God in the matter of prayer. I urge you to depend on the Holy Spirit who knows you and your individual personality, lifestyle, and schedule. It is He who will instruct you and show you the pathway of prayer that is right for you.

What time do I pray? Is early morning the only time to pray? If I don't get up early to pray, is it a sign I don't love God as much as others do? Is Satan interfering with my prayer life, stealing my time by making it difficult for me to get out of bed, or is God assigning me another time? Will God hear me at 10:00 a.m., at 1:00 p.m. or at 9:00 p.m. as quickly and clearly as He will at 5:00 a.m.? As you listen to the Spirit of God in your inner man, you will know the answers to these questions.

Satan is taking advantage of many believers with his subtlety. Praying out of a sense of guilt or according to another's standards can make prayer bondage rather than a privilege. For instance, if a person sleeps past his self-appointed hour of prayer, he can easily become consumed with his failure to get out of bed when the alarm sounds. The proverbial "fifteen minutes longer" gets in the way. A pattern of negative thinking can be immediately set in motion to play havoc with his prayer time. Also if, for some reason, his allotted prayer time is cut short, he feels guilty and his confidence in God can be shaken for that day. That's ridiculous thinking but Satan takes every advantage to stop prayer.

Does God command everyone to rise before daybreak to pray, regardless of individual and family lifestyles or job situations? I don't think so.

We do need to find time alone with the Father daily, whether it is early in the morning, in the middle of the afternoon, or late in the evening. It is easier for me if I begin my day with prayer. I love getting up before the world around me is awake. The first thing I do upon waking is to greet the Father, Jesus, and the Holy Spirit. The time is not as important as the heart attitude. The following are examples of two people I have known who spent time with the Father, fellowshipping with Him, and praying for others—yet they were totally different in their time and approach. One prayed until the joy of the Lord was released and the tears freely flowed down her face. She is my mother, the late Donnis Griffin.

After my dad retired from pastoral work he was always home and my mother realized she had to change her schedule to have time alone with God. In her frustration, she asked the Holy Spirit when she would ever find time to be alone with God again. Mother always said, "Don't ask God a question unless you want to know the answer." The Holy Spirit responded by telling her to get up and pray each morning while Buck (my dad) was out jogging. That was fine, except he was an early riser—one of those types who believes when you get up you are to be instantly awake all over—spirit, soul, and body.

Mother was a night owl and loved sleeping in but she was determined she would obey God. For a few mornings, at her request, my dad called her out of deep sleep before he left for his three mile run. But soon she found herself waking up without being prompted because the Lord had created a desire in her to get up and spend time in His presence. Her time alone with God was the most important time of her day. Early-morning prayer became a way of life for her even during those few years she was physically weak and could hardly pick up her Bible. The answers to her prayers were remarkable and prompted much thanksgiving to God the Father. As a result, her fellowship with God grew more and more intimate.

A gentleman friend of my parents, who lived in Atlanta Georgia, was used mightily by God to influence the lives of many people who frequented his place of business. He shared numerous testimonies of the power of God that he witnessed as a result of prayer and being obedient to the Spirit. Lives were changed; people received salvation and healing. If you asked this man to pray for you, you could know that at some point between nine and ten o'clock in the evening he was praying. Both my mother and my parents' friend have moved to heaven but I believe they are members of that great cloud of witnesses who are praying for us even today.

CONTINUALLY PRACTICE HIS PRESENCE

Jesus prayed all night and in the early morning, before ministering and after ministering. The Father's ears are open to the prayers of His people regardless of when we pray. Jesus said that we are to pray at all times[5], and Paul reinforced this teaching when he later wrote that we are to pray without ceasing (1 Thessalonians 5:17).

I once heard an expression that has become a part of my vocabulary: "Continually practice the presence of Jesus." The important thing is that you and I are to give the Lord preeminence in our lives. The Father is not limited to only certain hours of the day; He is always attentive to the prayers of His people. He never slumbers or sleeps.

"God is all the while effectually at work in you [energizing and creating in you the power and desire], both to will and to work for His good pleasure and satisfaction and delight" (Philippians 2:13 AMP). He will do His part; it is our responsibility to cooperate. "If you are willing and obedient, you shall eat the good of the land" (Isaiah 1:19 NKJV).

Prayer time is intended to be a time of joy in which you gain strength even while praying for others. When you are led by the Spirit in your prayer time, personal pressures are relieved rather than intensified.

You will have to make a decision to spend time in prayer. Effective praying does require a made-up mind, but it is not attained through sheer willpower. It is an activity that is motivated by the love of God, for God, and for others. It is in your prayer time where human weaknesses are often exposed, but always remember that

Jesus said, "My grace is sufficient for you, for my strength is made perfect in weakness" (2 Corinthians 12:9 NKJV). You can obey the call to prayer.

Satan would discourage you and steal your time with God, if possible. He suggests many ideas that are simply distractions. Ask the Holy Spirit for direction, obey Him, and God's grace will enable you to follow through at your divinely appointed prayer time. "Not that we are sufficient of ourselves to think of anything as being from ourselves, but our sufficiency is from God" (2 Corinthians 3:5 NKJV). It is His grace and ability at work in you motivating you to a life of prayer. It is His Word that lights your pathway and the Holy Spirit who takes the Words of Jesus and reveals them to you.

The disciples asked Jesus to teach them to pray. His teaching in Word and practice is our example for prayer today. Do not neglect your time alone with God in Bible study and prayer for this is the key to released power and praying prayers that avail much.

Many people in our Bible studies have listened to various teachers and struggled to pray earlier each morning and to intercede or to pray in the Spirit a set number of hours—following the routines of others. They have tried dividing their prayer time into so many minutes of worship, praise, personal confession, and intercession, but still feel frustrated because they haven't met someone's criteria. It causes much thanksgiving to God as we see these people set free—going from bondage to joy in their prayer time. Whom the Son has set free is free indeed! (John 8:36). Rejoice in your time with the Father God—whenever that time may be.

The following prayer will help you establish your commitment to pray:

PRAYERS THAT AVAIL MUCH®
TO PRAY

Father, in the name of Jesus, I thank You for calling me to be a fellow workman—a joint promoter and a laborer together—with You. I commit to pray and not to give up.

Jesus, You are the Son of God, and I will never stop trusting You. You are my High Priest, and You understand my weaknesses. So I come boldly to the throne of my gracious God. There I receive mercy and find grace to help when I need it.

There are times I do not know what I ought to pray for. Holy Spirit, I submit to Your leadership and thank You for interceding for us with groans that words cannot express. You search hearts and know the mind of the Spirit, because You intercede for the saints in accordance with God's will.

Therefore, I am assured and know that (with God being a partner in my labor) all things work together and are [fitting into a plan] for my good, because I love God and am called according to [His] design and purpose.

I resist the temptation to be anxious about anything, but in every circumstance and in everything by prayer and petition [definite requests] with thanksgiving continue to make my wants (and the wants of others) known to God. Whatever I ask for in prayer, I believe that it is granted to me, and I will receive it. Amen.

SCRIPTURE REFERENCES

1 Corinthians 3:9 NIV; Luke 18:1 NIV; Romans 8:26-27 NIV; Romans 8:28 AMP; Philippians 4:6 AMP; Mark 11:24 AMP

ANSWER THE CALL

1. Romans 8:14 says that if you are a son of God, you are led by the Spirit of God. How do you feel the Lord leads you? Has He led you to pray at a specific time?_____

_____

2. What does it mean to you to pray without ceasing (1 Thessalonians 5:17)? _____

_____

3. God does not want your prayer time to be drudgery but joy. What does God give you when it comes to prayer according to Philippians 2:13? _____

_____

_____

4. In 2 Corinthians 3:5 we find our sufficiency is from God. How does that affect your prayer life? _____

_____

CHAPTER 6
THE OVERTHROW
OF SATAN

May you be strengthened with all power, according to
his glorious might, for all endurance and patience with
joy, giving thanks to the Father, who has qualified us
to share in the inheritance of the saints in light. He
has delivered us from the dominion of darkness and
transferred us to the kingdom of his beloved Son, in
whom we have redemption, the forgiveness of sins.

Colossians 1:11-14 RSV

It is evident Satan is still at work to deceive, accuse, divide, and
conquer. However, the Church is a sleeping giant awakening
to the truth of the utter defeat of Satan.

Jesus spoiled principalities and powers, making a show of them
openly—exposing Satan to public shame (Colossians 2:15). In
Genesis 3:15 the Lord reveals the enemy would "bruise the heel"

(a metaphor for temporary suffering) of the Seed of the woman, while promising the Seed was to utterly crush and eternally defeat Satan. Little did Satan know the death of Jesus would be his own absolute defeat.

To successfully stand against the devil's rebel forces it is important to understand the victory was fought and won by our Redeemer who conquered Satan by dying for us. In Colossians 2:15, Paul reveals the absolute defeat of the devil by Jesus Christ: "And having disarmed the powers and authorities, he made a public spectacle of them, triumphing over them by the cross" (NIV).

Now, God, through Christ Jesus, through the cross, has already disarmed the enemy's principalities and powers. In 1 Corinthians 2:8, we find that had the prince of this world known what was going to happen, he would never have crucified the Son of God. With that crucifixion came Satan's defeat.

THE LOCATION OF JESUS

The Apostle Paul receives the divine revelation of how Jesus utterly defeated Satan, his principalities and powers and shares it in his letters to the churches, the epistles of the New Testament. This revelation helps us to understand where Jesus, the Church, and our archenemy are all located in the spirit realm in order to carry on strategic prayer assignments. In Ephesians 1:20-23 NIV Paul reveals the location of Jesus in referring to the power of God:

...which he exerted in Christ when he raised him from the dead and seated him at his right hand in the heavenly realms, far above all rule and authority, power and dominion, and every title that can be given, not only in the present age but also in the one to come. And God placed all things under his feet and appointed him to be head over everything for the church, which is his body, the fullness of him who fills everything in every way.

The physical location of the Lord Jesus today is at the right hand of the Father, where He sits in glory as the spiritual Head of the Church.

LOCATION OF THE CHURCH

It is also vital that we understand our spiritual location. In Ephesians 2, we find we were once children of disobedience, objects of wrath, under the control of the prince of the power of the air (Satan). We were powerless to deliver ourselves from this bondage. But God, who is rich in mercy, made us alive with Christ, raised us up with Him, and seated us with Him in the heavenly realms. (Ephesians 2:4-6.) We are located in *Christ!* Where is that? If we are truly in Him then we are seated *far above* all principality, and power, and might, and dominion and every name that is named not only in this world, but also in that which is to come. (Ephesians 1:20-21.) The good fight of faith is released from a high vantage point.

This elevated status does not put us in a position to lord it over people but in a position to stand firm against the demonic world in the spirit realm. It appears to me we already hold the keys to victory; we already have the victory since we are already seated with Christ in heavenly places, but learning to walk this out takes time and practice—a renewing of the mind. Satan is somewhere out there, and when we locate him, we find he is underneath the feet of Jesus, and we are His body. In Christ Jesus, Satan is under our feet. We have authority over him and his influences through prayer.

It seems almost too good to be true when we begin to comprehend the position of the Body of Christ—the Church. Often our mental image has been one that suggests Satan is just barely under our feet and we are actually treading on him. This is not the picture we get from Ephesians where we find that we are seated far above the satanic regime.

Our Lord won a decisive battle—not just a skirmish that gives us limited authority over the enemy, but a *total victory* that renders the devil paralyzed. (Hebrews 2:14-15.)

Even before the death and resurrection of Jesus, He sent His disciples out, saying, "Behold! I have given you authority and power to trample upon serpents and scorpions, and [physical and mental strength and ability] over all the power that the enemy [possesses]; and nothing shall in any way harm you" (Luke 10:19 AMP).

Jesus gives physical and mental strength and ability to carry out the work He began while here on earth. Jesus went about in towns and villages teaching in synagogues and preaching the Good News of the Kingdom and healing every disease and every weakness and infirmity among the people. (Matthew 4:23.) Then in John 14:12 He says to His disciples, "I tell you the truth, anyone who has faith in me will do what I have been doing. He will do even greater things than these, because I am going to the Father" (NIV).

You and I are to do the works of Jesus, knowing the prayers of a righteous man avail much. Jesus knew there would be opposition to the Gospel and His people would suffer persecution, but He wants us to know the defeat of Satan was effective and we are to keep it in effect.

THE LOCATION OF SATAN

Even before Jesus' death, burial, and resurrection He gave His disciples power over the enemy in His name. Are we to suppose that now, after the resurrection, the Church has less power than these men had before the cross? Never! How dare we continue to glorify the works of the devil with our proclamations and testimonies and, in some cases, our fears.

Satan is a defeated foe.

The prophet Isaiah says we will look at Satan and say, "Can this be the one who shook the earth and made the kingdoms of the world tremble?" (Isaiah 14:16 NLT). When we realize Satan's power and authority over the Church of the Lord Jesus have really been broken and put to naught, we will begin to be even more effective in our prayers.

We can see from the passage in Luke that Satan does not have authority over the children of God. His only weapon is deception through fear. Let's change our focus from the works of Satan to the wondrous works of God.

Great things He has done!

It was Nehemiah who said to the people of his day: "Don't be afraid of the enemy! Remember the Lord, who is great and glorious" (Nehemiah 4:14 NLT). If the Lord would help those under the Old Covenant, how much more would He desire to help us under the New Covenant? Not because He cares for us more than He cared for ancient Israel, whom He called the apple of His eye, but because of what was accomplished through the cross.

Hebrews 2:14-15 is an exciting, bold statement about Jesus Christ: "Since the children have flesh and blood, he too shared in their humanity so that by his death he might destroy him who holds the power of death—that is, the devil—and free those who all their lives were held in slavery by their fear of death" (NIV).

Jesus has made Satan of no effect, and has brought him to naught. Jesus paid a debt He did not owe. We could not get out of our bondage on our own, but Jesus came on our behalf. He dealt a fatal blow to Satan that made him of no effect, and delivered us out of bondage. That which was impossible with man was possible with God.

Satan works through deceit—through confusing the minds of people. In order to pursue destruction in the earth, he has to have human cooperation. To accomplish his earthly deeds, he needs physical bodies.

Sin begins with a thought. (James 1:14.) Where does discord begin in our homes and churches? It begins with a thought. When that thought is considered valid, we begin a progressive search to prove its validity. Thoughts against others; feelings of rejection, intimidation, insecurity; the belief that others are against us; high-minded attitudes which convince us that we are better than others, causing us to overestimate ourselves and underestimate others—all such mental activity is contrary to truth. The next thing we know we are speaking out what we are thinking, and those words begin to build fires among our co-workers, friends, and companions. Then everything gets out of hand and we can't imagine how it all began. The result of wrong thinking is strife and every evil work. (James 3:16.)

RESPONSIBILITY IN THE CHURCH

In 1 Peter 2:1-5 NKJV, the Apostle Peter shares with us the responsibility of believers as part of the Body of Christ:

Therefore, laying aside all malice, all deceit, hypocrisy, envy, and all evil speaking, as newborn babes, desire the pure milk of the word, that you may grow thereby, if indeed you have tasted that the Lord is gracious. Coming to Him as to a living stone, rejected indeed by men, but chosen by God and precious, you also, as living stones, are being built up a spiritual house, a holy priesthood, to offer up spiritual sacrifices acceptable to God through Jesus Christ.

As living stones we have a part to play in the Church of Jesus Christ. God did not create passive stones; He created lively stones. We are to exercise all the power He has given us in the spirit realm. Our heavenly Father has given us power to be creative in this world, to exert a positive influence, to make a difference in the cities and towns in which we are planted.

All of us are to make a difference in our churches, in our neighborhoods, and in our businesses and homes. I want to remind you once again that Jesus says the gates of hell shall not prevail against us. (Matthew 16:18.) Sometimes it looks as if God has got a lot to do to make that statement come true. Sometimes it looks as if the gates of hell are prevailing. That is when our faith comes into the picture. By faith we reach out and take hold of what Jesus says: *The gates of hell shall not prevail against you!*

This prayer is written to help you affirm your faith in God's ability in you and your authority over the enemy.

PRAYERS THAT AVAIL MUCH®

SPIRIT-CONTROLLED LIFE

Father, I pray for all saints everywhere. Help us remain teachable that we may receive instruction from the apostles, prophets, evangelists, pastors, and teachers. We will be Your children equipped for the work of the ministry, for the edifying of the Body of Christ. Bring us to the unity of faith and knowledge of the Son of God, to a perfect man, to the measure of the stature of the fullness of Christ.

Father, there is now no condemnation to those who walk according to the Spirit, because through Christ Jesus the law of the Spirit of life sets us free from the law of sin and death. Grant us the grace to live the life of the Spirit. Father, You condemned sin in the flesh [subdued, overcame, deprived it] of its power over us. Now the righteous and just requirement of the Law is fully met in us who live and move in the ways of the Spirit—our lives governed and controlled by the Holy Spirit.

On the authority of Your Word, we declare that we are more than conquerors and are gaining a surpassing victory through Jesus who loves us. We refuse to let ourselves be overcome with evil, but we will overcome and master evil with good. We have on the full armor of light, clothed with the Lord Jesus Christ, the Messiah, and make no provision for indulging the flesh.

May we always be doers of God's Word. We have God's wisdom, and we draw it forth with prayer. We are peace-loving, full of compassion and good fruits. We are free from doubts, wavering, and insincerity. We are subject to God, our Father.

We are strong in the Lord and the power of His might. Therefore, we take our stand against the devil and resist him; he flees from us. We draw close to God, and God draws close to us. We do not fear, for God never leaves us.

In Christ, we are filled with the Godhead: Father, Son, and Holy Spirit. Jesus is our Lord!

SCRIPTURE REFERENCES

Romans 8:2,4,9,14,31,37 AMP; Romans 12:21; James 1:22; James 3:17 AMP; Hebrews13:5; Ephesians 6:10; James 4:7,8; Colossians 2:10

ANSWER THE CALL

1. What does Colossians 2:15 reveal about the status of Satan?

_____

_____

2. When you read Ephesians 1:17-23, in what standing is the believer in Jesus Christ?_____

_____

_____

3. In Isaiah 14:16 we read that the day will come when we look at Satan in surprise realizing he was the one who made the kingdoms of the earth tremble. How does that affect your stance in prayer today?_____

_____

4. What is the result of wrong thinking according to James 3:16? Have you ever fallen prey to this deception? How can you avoid it in the future?_____

_____

5. When you read through 1 Peter 2:1-5, what do you feel your responsibility is as a part of the Body of Christ?_____

_____

CHAPTER 7
PURPOSE OF INTERCESSION

"This, then, is how you should pray:

'Our Father in heaven,

 hallowed be your name,

 your kingdom come,

 your will be done

  on earth as it is in heaven.

 Give us today our daily bread.

 Forgive us our debts,

 as we also have forgiven our debtors.

 And lead us not into temptation,

 but deliver us from the evil one.'"

Matthew 6:9-13 NIV

I n *Secrets of a Prayer Warrior* Derek Prince compares the kinds of prayer to musical instruments.[1] Just as an orchestra is made up of different instruments requiring diverse skills and abilities, our mingled kinds of prayer ascending to the heavens form an orchestra of prayer before the throne of God. He states, "Intercession is one of the highest arts of Christian life, one of the most difficult instruments to play. It requires a lot of practice, a lot of skill, a lot of maturity. To *intercede* means literally 'to come in between.' The intercessor is one who comes in between God and those for whom he is praying." (Ezekiel 22:30-31.)

The purpose of intercessory prayer is to establish the will of the Father in the earth. The true intercessor is listening for the will of God, watching and praying according to His will. The present-day prayer of Jesus issues from the right hand of the Father in heaven, and by His Spirit and His Word the prayer of intercession is imparted to our hearts. Heaven and earth unite as we unite in prayer with Jesus, an Intercessor who cannot fail. Ephesians 1:10 reveals God's ultimate purpose and the basis of our prayers: "That in the dispensation of the fulness of times he might gather together in one all things in Christ, both which are in heaven, and which are on earth; even in him."

Within the broad scope of His plan we can approach the Father on behalf of others, praying as He has instructed us, in order that we may lead a quiet and peaceable life and influence the lives of others. Through the medium of prayer we are instrumental in establishing the intercession of Jesus in the earth.

SPIRIT-LED INTERCESSION
BRINGS DELIVERANCE

Having finished a few household chores, I sat down with the folder of prayer requests. There were too many names to even mention; the requests that had come in were rather heavy. As I prepared to pray I contemplated how and where to start. I said aloud: "Father, I do not know where to begin today. There are so many needs in this world where we live. You know where intercession is most needed at this moment. I present my body to You as a living sacrifice, holy and acceptable unto You, which is my reasonable service and spiritual worship, to pray for whomever. Holy Spirit, according to Paul's teaching, You know the plan of God for today."

All of the Godhead is searching our hearts and the hearts of others. If you and I are willing, the Holy Spirit can bring us alongside another who needs spiritual assistance. The Spirit knows the very spot of the heaviest enemy attack and whose heart is crying out for freedom. (Romans 8:26-27.)

Prompted by the Holy Spirit, I began to use my weapon of praise, and after praying for a few minutes, I realized I was entering into that arena of prayer where the Holy Spirit "takes hold together with us" against our infirmities—our inability to produce results as the Scripture reveals in Romans 8:26. I did not even know for whom I was praying, much less the desired results.

In order for you to really appreciate this experience, I need to tell you that I had prayed for a young man named David and he was delivered from a lifestyle of addictions. Then after a period of time, he returned to his old habits. At that time I said indignantly: "Lord, for years I believed for this young man's release from his addictions. He was set free after he read the book of Malachi from *The Living Bible²* while sitting in his own living room all alone. He has given his testimony and witnessed for You, and now he is bringing a reproach to the Body of Christ. I am through. You will have to raise up another intercessor."

SPIRITUAL EYES OPENED

Aren't you glad God looks on the heart? As I continued to pray, I had a vision of myself standing before a building. It was obviously a business, and I recognized where I was because I had been there before. When I walked around the building I saw him. There stood David, engrossed in his work. He was totally unaware of three demonic spirits around his head. One had his fingers in David's ears, another had his hands over David's eyes, and the third had his arm around David's head as though he were binding something to his mind. My prayer armor was in place. (Ephesians 6:10-18.)

In my boldness, these three presented no problem to the Holy Spirit within me. Using the authority I had been given by the Lord Jesus over all the power of the satanic Kingdom, I began to speak to those spirits. (Luke 10:19.) As I gave them the command to go in the name of Jesus, they left one by one. As the Holy Spirit gave me utterance, I declared deliverance, peace, and restoration over this young man.

A few days later when I talked with David, I asked if God had been talking to him recently. He shared with me how he had not wanted to appear self-righteous and chose to share a joint with his friend. He believed he could "walk in the middle of the road," remaining a Christian yet taking a smoke when he wanted—after all, he could handle it now.

This kind of thinking is a snare of the enemy into which many Christians have fallen because of a lack of knowledge. David admitted, however, that lately he had become concerned because he realized he was no longer hearing the voice of God. He continued: "I woke up the other morning and saw that I was no longer in the middle of the road. I was not only over on the side, but I was off the shoulder and into the ditch. I had been confused about the voices that I was hearing and was no longer sure about what was true. This morning I heard God's voice and knew that it was the Lord speaking to me. I heard and understood truth."

Praise the name of Jesus; God gave me the grace to pray, and I saw the purpose of intercession in action when I cooperated with the Holy Spirit in prayer. All glory to the Father; it's by the grace of God I even desired to pray. Deliverance and restoration were accomplished—the prodigal son had come home. Yes, the Holy Spirit knew where the intercession was most needed that day. The result was a season of freedom that lasted for six years, but little did we know there was another test ahead that would take us into another time of even greater turbulent storms and separation.

PLEADING THE CAUSE OF OTHERS

Pleading the cause of others, as in a court case, is another purpose of intercession: "Therefore I exhort first of all that supplications, prayers, intercessions, and giving of thanks be made for all men" (1 Timothy 2:1 NKJV). Here again, Jesus is our example. Isaiah said of Him: "He bare the sin of many, and made intercession for the transgressors" (Isaiah 53:12).

When praying for others, it is important to unite with the Spirit who helps us prepare and plead our case on behalf of others. There is power in our words, and praying according to the will of God keeps us focused on God's promises. Jesus prays Peter's faith will not fail[3]; Paul prays for the saints when he hears of their faith[4]. Your prayers are to be led by the Spirit of God not by bad reports. It's important to pray the answer or promise of God's Word for your situation, not the problem. God already knows the problem.

It is imperative we have the intercession of Jesus revealed to us for those with whom we are emotionally involved, especially our loved ones. This is an area in which our own will and feelings can so easily come into play. When we react emotionally to a situation, allowing pride or emotions to control us, the picture becomes distorted and we may lose a sense of the proper manner in which to pray; sometimes we may even find ourselves seeking revenge in certain situations. This is contrary to the Word of God in Romans 12:19.

INTERCESSION AS DEFENSE
OR VINDICATION

Another purpose of intercession is to defend or vindicate someone or his or her actions. We cannot do this while holding anything against the person for whom we are praying. In order to pray for others, we must walk in forgiveness. Unforgiveness is the number one hindrance to answered prayer. (Mark 11:25.)

There was a period of time when I was having difficulty praying for one of our daughters. She had asked Jesus to come into her heart at an early age; later, in her teenage years she was baptized with the Holy Spirit. Since the time of her salvation experience, she had faithfully read her Bible. After she graduated from college, she was different, and I did not like what I was seeing.

While she was still in high school, God had performed a miracle in our relationship and healed our communication breakdown. The Spirit of God taught me how to pray for her. I wrote that prayer down and prayed it until the breakthrough came.

Not only were her attitudes changed, but God also taught me more about working out my own salvation with fear and trembling and, as a result, godly changes took place within me.

This was the same daughter who had prayed for her mom and dad when we were having a communication problem which looked hopeless: *Jesus is Mom and Dad's peace, and He has made both one, and has broken down the middle wall of partition between them. He has abolished in His flesh the enmity, to make in Himself of the two, one new man, so making peace. He has reconciled both unto God in one body by the cross, having slain the enmity thereby.* (Ephesians 2:14-16.)

She shared this prayer with me, and we prayed in agreement knowing Jesus says, "If two of you on earth agree about anything you ask for, it will be done for you by my Father in heaven" (Matthew 18:19 NIV).

It appeared now, however, that in her pursuit of money and pleasure, our daughter had forsaken all we had taught her, and God had very little space in her life. I began praying for her, but apparently to no avail. It would be several years before the barriers came down. God is faithful, and when you pray with a pure heart He hears and answers prayer.

One day my husband said to me, "You have grown very hard and unforgiving toward Terri. You need to forgive her and continue walking in love."

At first I refused to believe this was true, but God by His Spirit revealed to me that in order for my prayers on her behalf to have any effect, I had to acknowledge my unforgiveness and repent. He reminded me of John 20:23: "If you forgive anyone his sins, they are forgiven; if you do not forgive them, they are not forgiven" (NIV). I had never known how to apply this Scripture and was concerned about praying presumptuously or foolishly. It was my heart's desire to pray accurately and according to the intercession of Jesus.

First of all, I asked forgiveness for my attitude toward my daughter, and God was faithful and just to forgive me and cleanse me from all unrighteousness. (1 John 1:9.) Then the Holy Spirit led me to release Terri from her sins. I certainly did not want my child suffering the judgment pronounced on sin. I wanted her delivered.

My prayer for Terri was: "Father, I forgive her and according to Your Word her sins are forgiven. I no longer hold anything against her, and, according to Your Word, neither do You. Thank You for Your mercy and grace You give to us.

"Jesus, I thank You for coming into the world to seek and save Terri who has lost her way. Whether she goes to the highest heights or the lowest depths, Your Spirit goes with her. She has gone the way of transgressors, but You, oh Lord are making intercession for her. Have mercy upon this lost sheep and bring her back to the fold. If by any fault of our neglect, she has strayed from You, forgive us our mistakes and reveal Your unconditional love to Terri. Draw us all closer to You with cords and bands of love. Unite our family in love and abide in our hearts. Surely goodness and mercy shall follow us all the days of our lives and we shall dwell in the house of the Lord forever." (Psalm 23:6.)

Then I loosed the deception and lie of the enemy from Terri and released to her godly sorrow which works repentance to salvation (2 Corinthians 7:10) that she might receive life and that more abundantly (John 10:10). Then it was time to rejoice and give glory to God for His intervention in her life. She did awake to righteousness and returned to the Shepherd of her soul. Glory to God for the great things that He has done.

Intercession in Accordance With God's Will

God's Word is His Will. Our prayers in accordance with God's purpose and plan ascend into the Throne Room and are a sweet smelling savor to the Lord—He hears the prayers of His people. So often we jump in and begin praying in answer to a need without knowing what God says.

There was a time when Judah had committed the sin of idolatry. God tells Jeremiah he is not to pray for Judah, neither is he to lift up a cry for them nor make intercession for them. (Jeremiah 7:16.) Later, Jeremiah does intercede on their behalf, but his prayer is never answered.

There were times when God looked for a man to pray in order to withhold judgment, but it seems that it was not the will of the Father to withhold His judgment from Judah at this time.

In 1 John 5:16-17, John writes: "If any man see his brother sin a sin which is not unto death, he shall ask, and he shall give him life for them that sin not unto death. There is a sin unto death: I do not say that he shall pray for it. All unrighteousness is sin: and there is a sin not unto death."

Learn to recognize the voice of the Holy Spirit and allow Him to lead you in prayer. We can't just get upset with people and decide that we will withhold our intercession for them because we want to see them punished. Vengeance is God's decision: "Recompense to no man evil for evil...Vengeance is mine; I will repay, saith the Lord" (Romans 12:17, 19).

The joyous intercessor is always ready to release the mercy cry, "Father, forgive them; for they know not what they do" (Luke 23:34). Our cry is, "Lord, have mercy!"

COMMENDING OTHERS TO GOD

In intercession you may commend others to God. Commend means "to entrust for care or preservation."[5] In Hebrews 7:25 and Romans 8:26-28 we read that Jesus ever lives to make intercession for people. God's desire is that all men be saved and come to know the truth. (1 Timothy 2:4.) We commend to the Lord our loved ones, as well as others, for salvation, healing, reconciliation, and restoration. In intercessory prayer, by the grace of God, we furnish any kind of assistance or help necessary to establish the eternal plan of God in the earth, being profitable to His Kingdom, positively affecting individuals, communities, and nations. Our Lord cares about all people in all parts of the globe. My prayer is, "Lord, I ask You for the grace and desire to pray for those who do not yet know You."

There is so much to learn from those who have walked the pathway of prayer. As a young girl, St. Thérèsa of Lisieux, who gave her life to prayer after seeing a vision of Jesus on the Cross wrote:

"I was concerned not with the souls of priests but with those of great sinners which I wanted to snatch from the flames of hell."[6] In prayer we are always learning; it is truly an adventure with eternal significance. I encourage you to spend time in prayer and in study.

God's overall plan includes the restoration of all things, the manifestation of the sons of God and the fulfillment of His promises to Israel. (Romans 8-11.) God's purposes are eternal. We are preparing the way of the Lord as He sets the stage for the millennial reign of Christ.

O the depth of the riches both of the wisdom and knowledge of God! how unsearchable are his judgments, and his ways past finding out!

For who hath known the mind of the Lord? or who hath been his counsellor?

Or who hath first given to him, and it shall be recompensed unto him again?

For of him, and through him, and to him, are all things: to whom be glory for ever. Amen.

Romans 11:33-36

Continue in faith as a follower of Jesus, cooperating with God's plan, praying always without fainting or turning coward. God's eternal plan will be consummated.

STANDING AGAINST THE ENEMY

Over the years there have been those who shared how they were praying Old Testament scriptures against those who have mistreated them and their families. This is where we have to ask the Holy Spirit to help us rightly divide the Word of Truth, and as followers of Jesus we turn to His teachings.

Under the *Old Covenant*, King David considered the enemies of God to be his own personal enemies, and he physically annihilated as many of them as possible. The Old Testament way of dealing with those who opposed God was to execute God's vengeance and wrath upon them physically. When Jesus came to earth as a man, He brought grace and truth to the human race (John 1:17) and authority over the power of the devil (Luke 9:1). The *New Testament* saint administers his or her God-given authority in the spiritual realm, not the physical. Jesus taught us to love our enemies…to pray for them. (Matthew 5:44.) Ephesians 6 tells us how to stand against spiritual enemies today:

Put on the full armor of God, so that you will be able to stand firm against the schemes of the devil. For our struggle is not against flesh and blood, but against the rulers, against the powers, against the world forces of this darkness, against the spiritual forces of wickedness in the heavenly places. Therefore, take up the full armor of God, so that you will be able to resist in the evil day, and having done everything, to stand firm.

Ephesians 6:11-13 NASB

These verses do not tell us to "fight." We are to "stand firm" against the schemes of the devil and "resist" in the evil day, and having done all, stand firm. This is the time to let the high praises of God be in your mouth, and a two-edged sword in your hand to execute vengeance only upon the satanic kingdom. (Psalm 149:6-7.)

In Psalm 122:6 we are admonished to pray for the peace of Jerusalem. This holy city is an important destination today and will be in the millennial reign of Christ Jesus. Join me in praying for peace.

PRAYERS THAT AVAIL MUCH®
PEACE OF JERUSALEM

Father, in the name of Jesus and according to Your Word, I long and pray for the peace of Jerusalem, that its inhabitants may be born again. I pray that You, Lord, will be a refuge and a stronghold to the children of Israel. Father, Your Word says "multitudes, multitudes are in the valley of decision" and whoever calls upon Your name shall be delivered and saved.

Have mercy upon Israel and be gracious to them, O Lord, and consider that they fight for their land to be restored. You, Lord, are their Strength, and Stronghold in their day of trouble. We pray that they are righteous before You and that You will make even their enemies to be at peace with them. Your Word says You will deliver those for whom we intercede, who are not innocent, through the cleanness of our hands. May they realize that their defense and shield depend on You.

We thank You for Your Word, Lord, that You have a covenant with Israel and that You will take away their sin. They are Your beloved. Your Word also says that Your gifts are irrevocable, that You never withdraw them once they are given, and that You do not change Your mind about those to whom You give your grace or to whom You send Your call. Though they have been disobedient and rebellious toward You, Lord, we pray that now they will repent and obtain Your mercy and forgiveness through Your Son, Jesus. We praise You, Lord, for Your compassion and Your forgiveness to Your people. We praise You that they are under Your protection and divine guidance, that they are Your special possession, Your peculiar treasure, and that You will spare them; for we have read in Your Word that all Israel shall be saved!

Pray for the peace of Jerusalem! May they prosper that love you, "the Holy City"! Peace be within your walls and prosperity within your palaces. Amen.

SCRIPTURE REFERENCES

Joel 3:14; Job 22:30 AMP; Romans 11:29 AMP; Isaiah 45:17

ANSWER THE CALL

1. How would you define "intercession" in light of Ezekiel 22:30?_____

_____

_____

2. What does Ephesians 1:10 reveal about God's ultimate plan and purpose?_____

_____

3. In Luke 10:19-20, Jesus says He has given us authority over all the power of the enemy, but to rejoice that your name is written in heaven. How do these Scriptures change the way you feel about the effectiveness of your prayers? Does it refocus your motives?_____

_____

4. According to Mark 11:25, what is the number one hindrance to answered prayer? Are there any situations you need to deal with in this respect?_____

_____

_____

5. How does the Apostle Paul tell us to deal with feelings of revenge in Romans 12:17-19?_____

_____

_____

_____

6. In 1 Timothy 2:4, the Scripture says God wants all men to be saved and come to the knowledge of the truth. Who can your pray this Scripture over in your life?_____

_____

_____

CHAPTER 8
THE GOOD FIGHT OF FAITH

Timothy, my son, I give you this instruction in keeping
with the prophecies once made about you, so that by
following them you may fight the good fight, holding
on to faith and a good conscience. Some have rejected
these and so have shipwrecked their faith.

1 Timothy 1:18-19 NIV

Now we turn our attention to the subject of spiritual
warfare, also known as "the good fight of faith." Prayer
prepares us to wage a successful spiritual warfare, but "spiritual
warfare" by itself is not prayer. Spiritual warfare is a lifestyle of
standing, and having done all; we stand!

Prayer is not mystical or ethereal. God Himself is practical in
His instructions for living the more abundant life, which includes
communication with the Trinity through prayer. He has not left us

to wander aimlessly around, hoping to stumble onto proper prayer techniques. He is a loving Father who knows how to reveal His ways to those who will abide in His presence.

Assuredly there is "warfare" spoken of in the Bible. To wage this fight, which Paul calls a "good warfare," cling tightly to your faith in God's Word and maintain a clear conscience.[1]

Pastor Rick Renner expresses, "*Spiritual warfare is real!* We are commanded in Scripture to deal with the unseen, invisible forces that have been marshaled against us. We are commanded to 'cast out devils' (Mark 16:17) and to 'pull down the strongholds' of the mind (2 Corinthians 10:3-5). This is a part of our Christian responsibility toward the lost, the oppressed, and the demonized."[2]

SPIRITUAL WEAPONS

Paul speaks of this warfare in 2 Corinthians 10:3-4: "For though we live in the world, we do not wage war as the world does. The weapons we fight with are not the weapons of the world. On the contrary, they have divine power to demolish strongholds" (NIV).

These spiritual weapons are for the demolition of enemy strongholds—mental barriers and imaginations or human reasoning programmed by philosophy, religious dogmas, childish suppositions, and ideas fashioned after and adapted to this world's external, superficial customs. These proud arguments and obstacles are fortifications that have set themselves up against the knowledge of God in the minds of people.

I personally will use these spiritual weapons against every rebel who remains, after I have first used them on myself and I am surrendered to Christ. The true intercessor refuses to be conformed to this world, but is transformed by the renewing of his mind, that he "...may prove what is that good, and acceptable, and perfect, will of God" (Romans 12:2). This is required if we truly present our bodies as living sacrifices unto God, which is our reasonable service and worship. (Romans 12:1.) It is necessary to bring our thoughts into obedience to the Captain of our salvation.

Building Up Through Worship

It seems few people in the Body of Christ understand the prayer of worship. Worship is more than singing a few songs. Worship has to do with our attitude which is displayed in our everyday-going-to-work lifestyle. For instance, an attitude of humility can be witnessed in our words and actions. In his book, *Secrets of a Prayer Warrior*, Derek Prince says, "Worship, in a sense, is covering your face and your body. It is bowing low, bending the head. Of course, this does not have to be solely a description of the physical body; we are talking about something in the spirit—the approach of our spirits to God."[3]

God is looking for true worshippers—those who will worship Him in spirit and in truth. (John 4:24.) Worship keeps us secure in the secret place of the Most High:

A thousand may fall at your side, and ten thousand at your right hand, but it shall not come near you.

Only a spectator shall you be [yourself inaccessible in the secret place of the Most High] as you witness the reward of the wicked.

Because you have made the Lord your refuge, and the Most High your dwelling place,

There shall no evil befall you, nor any plague or calamity come near your tent.

Psalm 91:7-10 AMP

You do not have to be afraid of the enemy's tactics. Continually throughout the Word of God we read, "Do not fear," "Be not afraid," "Be of good courage." You do not have to fear demons will jump on you or attach themselves to you. Fear opens the door for demonic activity; faith is your shield that will "...quench all the flaming missiles of the wicked [one]" (Ephesians 6:16 AMP). You are inaccessible in the secret place of the Most High.

Maintain an attitude of worship by acknowledging the presence of God at all times, on every occasion, and your moral conduct will please the Father. His praise is to be continually in your mouth. Praise is a vocal adoration of God, while worship is an attitude.

RECOGNIZE THE ENEMY

There was a time when I treated my husband as though he were my enemy. This attitude was reflected in my behavior. Before I learned to pray prayers that avail much, I tried every tactic I knew to force him to go to church. After all, this was certainly the will of God. He needed to be a good example to our children and, besides that, I was tired of always feeling so alone.

Every Sunday morning the battleground was set. I would pray this would be the day my husband would arise and go to church with us. I would wake up the children, feed them breakfast, and see they were dressed properly, while my husband would remain in bed. At every opportunity I would run to the bedroom nagging, coercing, speaking gently, and screaming, among other things. Sometimes I would wake the children early and send them into the bedroom to wake Daddy.

One day the Holy Spirit said to me, "Since you have prayed, believe." The gentle voice of the Spirit instructed me to treat my husband just as I would if he were attending church. I realized my conduct had not been an example of the love of God, and remembered someone had said believing is acting as though God has heard and answered prayer. This is action added to faith.

Sunday mornings were certainly easier for the children and me once I changed my behavior through the grace given me by the Lord

Jesus. My prayers prevailed when I submitted to God, allowing Him to work His will in me. I waged the good fight of faith with praise and thanksgiving. I quit concentrating on my husband's behavior and turned my attention to developing a more intimate relationship with the Lover of my soul. In fact I no longer even thought about my husband's behavior and its affect on our children.

It was only a few weeks later I walked into the living room and saw my husband dressed, announcing he was going to church with us. God wanted to prove Himself mighty that He might be glorified!

THE DEVICES OF SATAN

In his book, *The Screwtape Letters*, C. S. Lewis wrote: "There are two equal and opposite errors into which our race can fall about the devils. One is to disbelieve in their existence. The other is to believe, and to feel an excessive and unhealthy interest in them."[4] Satan takes advantage of the believer who is unbalanced in his thinking and unstable in his ways. Either way leaves us open to his tactics. But, we do not have to be ignorant of Satan's devices. Ephesians 6:10-18, which describes our prayer armor and lists our weapons of prayer, exposes the enemy and his ranks. Paul begins in verse 10 by giving believers an exhortation to develop and exercise the courage necessary to resist and stand against the enemies of God: "Finally, my brethren, be strong in the Lord, and in the power of his might."

These unseen enemies are trying to turn us from the Lord; to create fear, doubt and unbelief; to induce us to be unfaithful to God's Word. Satan uses deceit, pressure and cunning craftiness as snares set to keep our attention on problems, provoking us to believe other people are to blame for our circumstances.

Our insecurities allow Satan to send us thoughts of accusation against people. Much too often we may cling to our unhealed hurts and unresolved personal issues. In an effort to protect ourselves, we may camouflage these deep crippling emotions with things the Lord hates. Proverbs 6 gives us a list: "...a proud look, a lying tongue, hands that shed innocent blood, a heart that devises wicked plans, feet that are swift in running to evil, a false witness who speaks lies" (6:17-19 NKJV). We have the necessary weapons to pull down strongholds of suspicion, unforgiveness, distrust that incites us to hurl accusations at one another, and discord among the brethren. We have been called to freedom but we do not allow freedom to become an incentive to our flesh or an excuse for selfishness, but through love we serve one another. (Galatians 5:13.)

Satan's greatest delight is to disturb harmony through deception. One of his favorite ploys is heaping condemnation on the believer, turning him against himself. Paul makes it clear that we are not to be against one another or ourselves, but against spiritual rebels in heavenly places.

WRESTLING AGAINST
SPIRITUAL ENEMIES

"Finally, be strong in the Lord and in the strength of His might. Put on the full armor of God, so that you will be able to stand firm against the schemes of the devil. For our struggle is not against flesh and blood, but against the rulers, against the powers, against the world forces of this darkness, against the spiritual forces of wickedness in the heavenly places" (Ephesians 6:10-12 NASB). Jesus knew that there would be people who would set themselves against the Word of God, which we preach. Yet He said to us, "Love your enemies, bless them that curse you, do good to them that hate you, and pray for them which despitefully use you, and persecute you" (Matthew 5:44). Our Lord was never against a person, only against the evil one who holds people in bondage.

Paul's writings are in harmony with the teachings of Jesus. In his writings in Ephesians 6 in the King James Version, he says that we are "not to wrestle" against people, or to set ourselves against them, but that our struggle is against Satan and his regime. So, what is the practical application of this Scripture? How does one wrestle with the devil or struggle against him?

One day while searching for the true meaning of this word translated "wrestle," in *Vine's Expository Dictionary* I came across two seemingly insignificant shades of meaning: "sway" and "vibrate." Mr. Vine wrote: "...wrestling...is used figuratively, in Ephesians 6:12, of the spiritual conflict engaged in by believers." [5]

The two synonyms given made no sense to me. I tried out, "We *sway* not against flesh and blood," then, "We *vibrate* not against flesh and blood." It appeared that these two words simply did not work in that context.

Finally, I turned to Webster's dictionary, and discovered that *sway* means "to swing slowly and rhythmically back and forth from a base or pivot — to fluctuate or veer between one point, position, or opinion and another."[6] Some believers try to function in this mindset, swaying back and forth between different kinds of teaching, or being "double minded" as James called it (James 1:8), and thus receiving nothing from God. They grow weary in their prayer life and many of them faint in their minds.

However, there is another meaning of this word *sway*. It also means "a controlling influence; sovereign power; dominion; the ability to exercise influence or authority; dominance."[7] Therefore to sway means, "to rule over, control, dominate, or prevail."

According to Ephesians 1:20-22, we believers are seated in heavenly places in Christ *far above* the earthly realm. Yes, there is spiritual warfare going on all around us, but we hold sway over Satan and his forces. In the name of Jesus, we have the authority, power, might, and strength to cause Satan to turn from a given course.

Isn't that what we are trying to do in spiritual warfare—to turn the course of Satan, to divert him from that which he has plotted and planned against the Body of Christ? In spiritual warfare we hold sway over him, not over human beings; we have authority and control over principalities, powers, the rulers of the darkness of this world, and spiritual wickedness in heavenly places. (Ephesians 6:10-12.)

In one place the psalmist says that it's as though we were dreaming (Psalm 126:1). It is almost too good to be true, but you and I have power and authority over the evil one.

It's time for us to stop focusing on the wiles of the devil and acknowledge we are sons and daughters of the Most High God enforcing the triumphant victory Jesus won for us. Spiritual warfare takes place in the mind of the believer and the battle is won through prayer and renewing our mind.

LIGHT THAT DISPELS
THE DARKNESS

What about the word "vibrate?" According to Webster it means "to give off light or sound by vibration."[8] A vibration is an emotional quality or supernatural emanation that is sensed by another person or thing.

The world talks about walking into a room and sensing "vibes." I know havoc has to take place in the seat of Satan's empire as we believers stand clothed in the armor of light, praying all manner of prayer. Light dispels darkness: "And the Light shines on in the darkness, for the darkness has never overpowered it [put it out or absorbed it or appropriated it, and is unreceptive to it]" (John 1:5 AMP). Jesus says to His disciples, "Ye are the light of the world" (Matthew 5:14). Paul writes, "For once you were darkness, but now you are light in the Lord; walk as children of light"[9] (Ephesians 5:8 AMP).

Another meaning of *vibrate* is "to vacillate or waver as between two opinions"[9] (i.e., between belief and doubt, faith and fear.) This frustrates the purposes and plans of God's prayer agenda. Swaying or vacillating between two opinions is the result of the presence of strongholds which have not yet been pulled down: "...the weapons of our warfare are not carnal, but mighty through God to the pulling down of strong holds" (2 Corinthians 10:4).

How do we "sway" and "vibrate" against spiritual rebels? It's by putting on the whole armor of God and "praying at all times [on every occasion, in every season] in the Spirit, with all manner of prayer and entreaty" (Ephesians 6:18 AMP). By speaking God's Word and praying with the understanding that God's Word is our sword, when the enemy comes to destroy our homes, churches and communities, we remind him of his defeat at Calvary by affirming God's Word over everything that concerns us.

The entrance of God's Word brings light, dispelling darkness. (Psalm 119:130.) When Jesus is confronted by Satan in Luke 4, He declares, "It is written," quoting from the Old Testament Scriptures. Turn to the Word of God for answers. Affirm the Word in your meditation and through prayer. There is no better prayer book than the Bible. God is watching over His Word to perform it. (Jeremiah 1:12.)

The following prayer is written to help you release your faith to stand against the enemy. It's a powerful prayer to affirm your position in Christ, especially when used on a daily basis.

PRAYERS THAT AVAIL MUCH®
To Put On the Armor of God

In the name of Jesus, I put on the whole armor of God, that I may be able to stand against the wiles of the devil; for I wrestle not against flesh and blood, but against principalities, powers, the rulers of the darkness of this world, and spiritual wickedness in high places.

Therefore, I take unto myself the whole armor of God, that I may be able to withstand in the evil day, and having done all, to stand. I stand, therefore, wearing the belt of truth. Your Word, Lord, which is truth, contains all the weapons of my warfare, which are not carnal, but mighty through God to the pulling down of strongholds.

I have on the breastplate of righteousness, which is faith and love. My feet are shod with the preparation of the Gospel of peace. In Christ Jesus I have peace and pursue peace with all men. I am a minister of reconciliation, proclaiming the good news of the Gospel.

I take the shield of faith, wherewith I am able to quench all the fiery darts of the wicked; the helmet of salvation *(holding the thoughts, feelings, and purpose of God's heart)*; and the sword of the

Spirit, which is the Word of God. In the face of all trials, tests, temptations, and tribulation, I cut to pieces the snare of the enemy by speaking the Word of God. Greater is He that is in me than he that is in the world.

Thank you, Father, for the armor. I will pray at all times—on every occasion, in every season—in the Spirit, with all [manner of] prayer and entreaty. To that end I will keep alert and watch with strong purpose and perseverance, interceding in behalf of all the saints. My power and ability and sufficiency are from God who has qualified me as a minister and dispenser of a new covenant [of salvation through Christ]. Amen.

SCRIPTURE REFERENCES

Ephesians 6:11-14; John 17:17; 2 Corinthians 10:4; Ephesians 6:14-15 AMP, Ephesians 2:14; Psalm 34:14;2 Corinthians 5:18; Ephesians 6:16-17 AMP; 1 John 4:4; 2 Corinthians 3:5-6 AMP

ANSWER THE CALL

1. In 2 Corinthians 10:3-5 we find that we are not to wage war as the world does. How are we to wage war?_____

_____

_____

2. What does it mean to you to worship the Lord in spirit and in truth (John 4:24)?_____

_____

_____

3. Jesus says in Matthew 5:44 we are to love our enemies and do good to them that hate us. Ephesians 6 makes it clear our battle is not with people; we are in a spiritual battle. In light of these Scriptures, a good thing you can do to someone who comes against you is pray for them. Who can you pray for today?_____

_____

_____

4. How does putting on the full armor of God (Ephesians 6:10-18) change how you feel about yourself?_____

_____

_____

CHAPTER 9
PRAYER STRATEGY

"So too the [Holy] Spirit comes to our aid and bears us up in our weakness; for we do not know what prayer to offer nor how to offer it worthily as we ought, but the Spirit Himself goes to meet our supplication and pleads in our behalf with unspeakable yearnings and groanings too deep for utterance. And He Who searches the hearts of men knows what is in the mind of the [Holy] Spirit [what His intent is], because the Spirit intercedes and pleads [before God] in behalf of the saints according to and in harmony with God's will."

Romans 8:26-27 AMP

Praying is a spiritual business to be practiced according to God's plan. As we have read in Ephesians 6 there are varying types of prayer or as stated in verse eighteen, "all manner of prayer and entreaty." The Holy Spirit knows the particular prayer strategy that is needed for any given situation. When we submit to His control, we will pray the appropriate prayer whether it is entreaty, supplication, petition, intercession, or thanksgiving.

The prayer of supplication is mentioned more in Scripture than intercession, yet we don't hear much about it. Easton's Illustrated Dictionary says of "effectual prayer" in James 5:16: "The Revised Version renders appropriately: 'The supplication of a righteous man availeth much in its working', i.e., 'it moves the hand of Him who moves the world.'"[1] That's a powerful statement. Our prayers make a difference. Take the time to learn the various forms of prayer, but even if you don't understand them all, the Holy Spirit is your teacher and will lead you in your prayer strategy.

THE BATTLE IS THE LORD'S

The book of Nehemiah reveals the need for the appropriate strategy. After hearing about the needs of his people and the broken walls of Jerusalem, Nehemiah leaves his prominent position as the royal cup-bearer in the Persian court and goes to Jerusalem.

He plans and persuades the people to rebuild the walls of the holy city, and while they build the walls, the Lord fights their battles. Every builder has his sword girded by his side, and so he works. They are ready to answer the sound of the trumpet. Likewise, we are equipped, ready to answer the call to prayer.

Today, just as in Nehemiah's time, the battle is the Lord's. Since that era Jesus has come alive on the pages of history, establishing the overthrow of Satan. If this is true, why do we have to wage any kind of spiritual warfare, and what is the nature of this warfare?

Sometimes wars were fought to obtain certain rights and establish certain laws. Our victory has already been won. God's laws are already on the books. In a sense you and I are like the governing civil authorities that enforce these laws of the land. It is our responsibility to stand against all enemies who would resist and set themselves up in opposition to God's laws. God has delegated to us the power and authority to enforce His divine will in the earth.

The policeman, for example, has delegated power and authority. He is not a terror to people of good conduct, but to those who break the law, he is something to be feared. Satan and his subjects are the lawless spirits who are constantly trying to overthrow the Kingdom of God. It is this enemy that is terrified of the children of God who know their delegated power and authority—those who understand the power in the name of Jesus.

Satan's reign as the prince of the power of the air is only for a season; he keeps attempting to overthrow the Kingdom of God with guerrilla warfare through deception. Sometimes we have to address these enemy forces just as Jesus did when the devil tempted Him. Jesus is our example. He responded to temptation by declaring the written Word of God. Today, we are the administrators of the victory which was won by our Lord and Savior Jesus Christ when

He spoiled principalities and powers, making a show of them openly. (Colossians 2:15.) As spiritual administrators, we are to walk in the ways of our Commander.

A Priesthood Which Has Obtained Mercy

As believers, you and I are to God a holy and royal priesthood which has obtained mercy. 1 Peter 2:9-10 tells us:

But ye are a chosen generation, a royal priesthood, an holy nation, a peculiar people; that ye should shew forth the praises of him who hath called you out of darkness into his marvellous light;

Which in time past were not a people, but are now the people of God: which had not obtained mercy, but now have obtained mercy.

We have obtained God's mercy in time of our need. I know you can look back through your life and see how often the mercy of God was extended to you. You perhaps weren't even aware God was looking out for you.

Because of God's mercy and His grace, we are here today seeking to know more about Him and His workings. Through Jesus you and I have obtained mercy and are admonished to be merciful. Jesus rebuked James and John when they wanted to call down fire from heaven upon a village that would not welcome or receive Him. (Luke 9:53-56.) Isn't this the feeling we have many times when praying for loved ones who do not seem to be responding to the Gospel? God does not want us to call down destruction and calamity on those for whom we pray. Instead, we are to release God's mercy, drawing sinners to Him with bands of love.

MANIFESTING MERCY AND PATIENCE

In the first chapter of the Book of Romans after his characterization of apostates, Paul uttered a profound rebuke, which I believe we are to heed. It appears to be a plea for the believer to show mercy rather than disdain and contempt for heretics.

Certainly ungodliness is inexcusable and God's judgment is against sin, but He is not against the sinner. Otherwise I wouldn't be here writing about prayer based on a relationship. Praise God! He was merciful and patient toward us while we were yet His enemies. (Romans 5:8.) Now, He is requesting that we manifest that same mercy and patience to others. Paul writes on this subject:

"Well," you may be saying, "what terrible people you have been talking about!" But wait a minute! You are just as bad. When you say they are wicked and should be punished, you are talking about yourselves, for you do these same things. And we know that

God, in justice, will punish anyone who does such things as these. Do you think that God will judge and condemn others for doing them and overlook you when you do them, too? Don't you realize how patient he is being with you? Or don't you care? Can't you see that he has been waiting all this time without punishing you, to give you time to turn from your sin? His kindness is meant to lead you to repentance.

Romans 2:1-4 TLB

In Romans 3, Paul continues to build his dissertation with this statement: "For all have sinned, and come short of the glory of God" (Romans 3:23). How can we afford to withhold mercy when we were once blind in our sins and in bondage to the god of this world?

Anyone who responds to the goodness of Jesus can be declared "not guilty." All can be saved in this manner by trusting Him to cleanse them from sin. We can all be justified freely by His grace. In Matthew 5:7, Jesus says, "Blessed are the merciful: for they shall obtain mercy."

It is impossible to pray effectively for those we are yet holding in contempt. Let go of a wrong detrimental attitude and cry, "Father, forgive them; they know not what they do." Release the mercy of God to those for whom you pray—not judgment and condemnation. Aren't we all in need of God's mercies that are new every morning?[2]

INTERCEDING FOR A LOVED ONE

When I first began to pray for our son's deliverance from the drug scene, I had little understanding about praying for a third party. I applied the rules, as I had been taught, governing the prayer of faith to the prayer of intercession.

I had been taught that if I prayed more than once for anything, I was praying in doubt and unbelief. However, the Holy Spirit had placed my son David upon my heart and I found myself praying for him again and again. It is possible for a mother's natural love to turn into unforgiveness, but the love of God will sustain her, enabling her to forgive again and again. A parent's emotions run the gamut from feelings of intense love to feelings of overwhelming acrimony. Sometimes a mother's prayers will be very objective—other times they will be filled with fervent, passionate longing to see that child cleansed by the blood of Jesus.

When praying for a loved one, it is imperative you admit to yourself and the Father the emotional hurts, disappointments, fears, and anger which are often denied. Denial of these emotional feelings hinders answered prayer.

There were times when circumstances looked good and I relaxed my supplication and intercession for David, only to have to go back and pray him out of adverse circumstances again. In moments of anger I declared I would never pray for him again, only to find myself drawn once more by the Holy Spirit to a place of fervent prayer and travail. Such intense intercession is a time for speaking truly and living truly—casting down imaginations and lofty things that seek to exalt themselves above the knowledge of God. (2 Corinthians 10:5.)

REPEATED INTERCESSION

One morning while I was praying I had a vision of a hedge made up of people and angels with flaming swords surrounding David. Yet I still could not understand why the same prayers had to be repeated. It was in the Book of Nehemiah where the Father revealed to me how an addictive person can continually bounce back and forth from compulsive behavior to freedom until he receives emotional wholeness enabling him to overcome toxic addiction.

While Nehemiah is working on the wall, his enemies gather together, calling him to come down to the plain of Ono and reason with them. But he refuses, saying, "I am doing a great work, so that I cannot come down" (Nehemiah 6:3). Nehemiah made a decision that kept him safe.

However, David's reaction to his tempters was quite different. Our prayers did not override David's free will, and God understood David's journey here on earth even though I didn't. When he would go down to the enemy territory, it was the intercession of the saints that would throw out the net of love and draw him back within the hedge again. Most of my prayers for him became prayers of thanksgiving, praise, and adoration to the One who loves my son even more than I do.

Often the Holy Spirit alerts me to a need for a particular prayer strategy. The Living Bible Paraphrase says it so well: "I remember that it is true that I am an ordinary, weak human being, but I don't use human plans and methods to win my battles. I use God's mighty weapons, not those made by men, to knock down the devil's strongholds. These weapons can break down every proud argument against God and every wall that can be built to keep men from finding him. With these weapons I can capture rebels and bring them back to God and change them into men whose hearts' desire is obedience to Christ" (2 Corinthians 10:3-5 TLB). We don't give up—God is able and willing to give us another start.

It is necessary to pull down strongholds that would set themselves against the knowledge of God. When I set myself to persevere in prayer for our son, I found myself in a spiritual battle—a tug of war. Satan does not want to relinquish even one individual he is holding in bondage. Reasoning with David only made him more stubborn. He resolved that his parents would not tell him how to live his life. He was a rock and nothing could move him. It was as though his intellect had flown the coop, and we heard statements that defied logic.

Obviously, David had taken leave of his senses—he was no longer in his right mind. Was this the son we loved and raised? Many times it appeared that the enemy had won. But I know in Whom I have believed and I am persuaded that my household shall be saved.

In Matthew 18, Jesus gives the keys of binding and loosing to the church, but for a long time I didn't understand how to use these keys effectively. If binding the devil works or if loosing the devil works, he should have been bound and loosed most definitely because I did both with much fervency. God will move heaven and earth to give you the understanding concerning the necessary spiritual weapons for the needed prayer strategy. I just kept seeking for answers, and He brought them across my path.

In *Shattering Your Strongholds,* Liberty Savard gives a basic outline for binding and loosing prayers for your unsaved loved ones. She writes:

To hold them steady, I bind (the positive, helpful side of binding) the individual to the will of God, the truth, the blood of Jesus, the mind of Christ and the work of the cross. I bind the strong man, Satan, (the negative, restraining side of binding) and then loose, crush, destroy, shatter, melt, and tear apart all hindrances, devices and influences he is trying to bring against the individual.

The next step is to tear down the strongholds in the lives of the captives. This is vital to keep them from cooperating with the enemy's attempts to recapture them. You can pull them out of the fire, but you have to continue loosing their strongholds to keep them from voluntarily returning there. Continue loosing until the Holy Spirit reveals they have begun to take over the reins of their own deliverance.

Continue to build up the wall and stand in the gap before God. Don't turn coward, lose heart and give up! All things are possible to him who believes. If your faith seems weak, cry out, "Lord, help my unbelief." He will help you. He sent the Holy Spirit to be your Strengthener and Standby. He is interceding.[3]

The words you speak are creative and will not return to God void.[4] Never be moved by good or bad circumstances, but keep your anchor firmly grounded in the Word of God. Remain steady regardless of the situation. Don't give up your position of priesthood or abort the mission which God has placed on your heart. You will know through the witness of the Holy Spirit when you have fulfilled your assignment. There will be a definite release within you—a knowing that you have to experience personally in order to completely understand. When you pray to extend forgiveness, and having done all to stand, stand giving glory to God.

A BURDEN FOR PRAYER

When I was a teenager, I remember well an incident that explains a temporary "burden" for prayer.

Our family had gone to visit my grandparents and on returning home we had a brush with death. The next day one of the church members called my dad to inquire if our lives had been in danger at a certain moment. When we were in trouble, the man said it was about that same time God had awakened him, and our faces had flashed before him as he prayed with groanings in the Spirit.

In this case, the Father found someone who responded to His call, someone who was faithful to pray, protecting us from an accident that could have snuffed out our lives. This man fulfilled his role as a priest unto God on behalf of his pastor and his family in time of crisis.

God wants your prayer time devoted to situations outside of your own personal problems. When you spend time with the Father in prayer and reading his Word, you will develop the mind of Christ. (Philippians 2:5.) In 1 Corinthians 2:16 the Apostle Paul says we have the mind of Christ and hold the thoughts, feelings, and purposes of His heart. When we search our inner man, we find what Christ would have us do.

A Sweet-Smelling Fragrance

In the tabernacle, in Old Testament worship, was the altar of incense that was placed before the ark of the testimony. Incense was burned upon the altar morning and evening. It was symbolic of acceptable prayers.

In the New Testament, this altar is now placed just before the throne of God. When you come before God, you come into His throne room, presenting yourself before His throne. Your prayers are a sweet-smelling fragrance before God. They are a perpetual and continual flow before the Lord, because prayer is persevering. Jesus said to pray without ceasing. Every prayer you have ever prayed is in the throne room as incense before the Lord.

BROADEN YOUR VISION

The Holy Spirit desires to broaden the scope of your prayer life. The Father has a plan for mankind and He desires that you become involved in that plan. He wants you to expand your prayer borders beyond the confines of your home and your local church. (However, do not neglect these vital areas of prayer.)

In Psalm 2:8 the Father says: "Ask of me, and I shall give thee the heathen for thine inheritance, and the uttermost parts of the earth for thy possession." Broaden your vision. Allow the Lord to imprint His intercession on the tablets of your heart—delegating prayer assignments to you as He wills. He wants you to become Kingdom-minded in preparation for the return of Jesus. Expand your prayer vision to include nations. Go global and get beyond the needs of your family as well as those prayer situations in the local church.

Remember the problems people often deal with originate in the spiritual realm and affect the soul, resulting in various forms of behavior even within your own life. Pray for the will of God to be done on earth as it is in heaven. Do not allow problems to dictate your prayer life. As you carry out your prayer assignments, submit to the leadership of the Spirit of God. Whether it is for the family, the church, the community or the nation, remain faithful to your assigned prayer burden until it is fulfilled.

AGREE WITH THE PLANS AND PURPOSES OF GOD

Involve yourself in the things Jesus is doing. You were destined from the beginning to be molded into the image of God's Son. (Romans 8:29.) Act like Jesus. Walk like Jesus. Talk like Jesus. Adopt the same attitude and purpose, which was in Christ Jesus. (Philippians 2:5.) In His present-day ministry, Jesus is the High Priest who intercedes before the Father God:

> Seeing then that we have a great high priest, that is passed into the heavens, Jesus the Son of God, let us hold fast our profession.
>
> Hebrews 4:14

In Greek, the word translated "profession" is *homologia*, which means, "whom we profess to be ours; profession [confession]."[5] Let us meet the terms of surrender to God whom we profess to be ours by affirming our faith in Him and His Word. This requires agreement with the plans and purposes of God. Jesus understands what we are going through and knows how to intercede for each situation. As you agree with His will, power is released.

> For we have not an high priest which cannot be touched with the feeling of our infirmities; but was in all points tempted like as we are, yet without sin.
>
> Hebrews 4:15

According to W.E. Vine, *infirmities* means, "want of strength... weakness...inability to produce results."[6] Many times in prayer we experience an inability to produce results, but Jesus is touched with these infirmities. According to Matthew 8:17, He bore these weaknesses and in Romans 8:26 we find that He and the Father sent a Helper who takes hold together with us against these inabilities in order to produce results. Jesus has made us "kings and priests" unto God the Father. (Revelation 1:6.)

As New Covenant believers, you and I are part of a "holy priesthood" offering "up spiritual sacrifices, acceptable to God by Jesus Christ" and a "royal priesthood" that we should show forth the praises of Him who has called us out of darkness into His marvelous light. (1 Peter 2:5, 9.) The first ministry of a New Testament priest is to offer up praises to God; the second is to declare His wonderful salvation through a life that emulates Jesus.

We enter into agreement with our High Priest who is praying at the right hand of the Father.

A Successful Prayer Life

Examination of the lives of prominent Christian men and women reveals they were, and are, men and women of prayer. They have a deep relationship with God. Jesus, throughout the New Testament, gives believers a pattern for successful living which includes a consistent prayer life. And in the Old Testament, the Song of Solomon shows a type of how close our relationship with Christ should be. This passage of Scripture calls us into a wonderful relationship with our Lord. The bridegroom (representing Christ) is saying to his beloved bride (representing us):

...Arise, my love, my fair one, and come away.

...let me see your face, let me hear your voice; for your voice is sweet and your face is lovely.

2:13-14 AMP

This is the call of Jesus to the Church today: "Arise, come apart, come away with Me." Everyone who spends time with Jesus discovers divine plans and purposes for their life: "The LORD confides in those who fear him; he makes his covenant known to them" (Psalm 25:14 NIV). What has God placed on your heart? The Christian's prayer armor is of the Spirit and God has written certain prayer ventures on your breastplate.

A sincere desire to have a successful prayer life necessitates looking beyond situations, problems, and circumstances. Don't be afraid of prayer burdens. Jesus says, "...my yoke is easy, and my burden is light" (Matthew 11:30). The Apostle Paul encourages us that those things we can see are only temporary and subject to change:

> For our light affliction, which is but for a moment, worketh for us a far more exceeding and eternal weight of glory;
>
> While we look not at the things which are seen, but at the things which are not seen: for the things which are seen are temporal; but the things which are not seen are eternal.
>
> 2 Corinthians 4:17-18

Situations in this world are constantly changing, but the things of the Spirit are unchanging. Involve yourself with the intercession of Jesus. Become utterly one with Him.

JESUS, OUR FOUNDATION

God said His house would be called a house of prayer. (Isaiah 56:7, Matthew 21:13.) You and I are that habitation (that house) with a firm and sure foundation. In 1 Corinthians 3:11, we find no man can lay a foundation other than the one that is laid, Jesus Christ. So, as our Foundation and High Priest, Jesus is our backing for all prayer including spiritual warfare.

The Church was a mystery in the Old Testament, but today we are the Church. Isaiah prophesies about the Church when he says:

Therefore thus says the Lord GOD,

"Behold, I am laying in Zion a stone, a tested stone, a costly cornerstone for the foundation, firmly placed..."

Isaiah 28:16 NASB

Jesus, our Foundation and Builder, says of the Church, "The gates of hell shall not prevail against it" (Matthew 16:18). Hallelujah! When we enter a spiritual battle we are not trying to obtain the victory. God has given us the victory, "and this is the victory that overcometh the world, even our faith" (1 John 5:4).

You are ready to assume your responsibility in the household of faith, knowing that you are a winner—more than a conqueror—called to a lifestyle of prayer. You belong to a holy and royal priesthood.

The prayer to follow will help you release your faith to develop the mind of Christ within you.

PRAYERS THAT AVAIL MUCH®
TO BE GOD-INSIDE MINDED

I am a spirit learning to live in a natural world. I have a soul, and I live in a physical body. I am in the world, but I am not of the world. God of peace, I ask You to sanctify me in every way, and may my whole spirit and soul and body be kept blameless until that day when our Lord Jesus Christ comes again. Father, You called me, and You are completely dependable. You said it, and You will do this. Thank You for the Spirit who guides me into all truth through my regenerated human spirit.

Lord, Your searchlight penetrates my human spirit, exposing every hidden motive. You actually gave me Your Spirit (not the world's spirit) so I can know the wonderful things You have given us. I am a child of God, born of the Spirit of God, filled with the Spirit of God, and led by the Spirit of God. I listen to my heart as I look to the Spirit inside me.

Thank you, Holy Spirit, for directing me and illuminating my mind. You lead me in the way I should go in all the affairs of life. You lead me by an inward witness. The eyes of my understanding are being enlightened. Wisdom is in my inward parts. God's love is perfected in me. I have an unction from the Holy One.

Father, I am becoming spirit-conscious. I listen to the voice of my spirit and obey what my spirit tells me. My spirit is controlled by the Holy Spirit and dominates me, for I walk not after the flesh, but after the spirit. I examine my leading in the light of the Word, in Jesus' name, Amen.

SCRIPTURE REFERENCES

1 Thessalonians 5:23, 24; John 16:13; Proverbs 20:27 NLT; 1 Corinthians 2:12 NLT; Romans 8:14, 16; John 3:6, 7; Ephesians 5:18; Isaiah 48:17; Ephesians 1:18; 1 John 4:12; 1 John 2:20; Romans 8:1

ANSWER THE CALL

1. Colossians 2:15 says Jesus spoiled the evil principalities and powers in the spirit realm. If the devil has been defeated, why is there still evil in the world and what is our goal in prayer?_____

_____

2. Matthew 5:7 says those who are merciful will receive mercy. With that Scripture in mind, how should you pray for others?_____

_____

3. The Apostle Paul shares about spiritual warfare in 2 Corinthians 10:3-5.What do these Scriptures say we have the ability to pull down through prayer? When praying for others, is it something we may have to do more than once? Why?_____

_____

_____

4. In Psalm 2:8, we find we can ask for the unsaved for our inheritance. Is there a nation on your heart you can pray for using this Scripture? If not, ask the Lord to expand your vision for the salvation of a nation. _____

_____

_____

5. What encouragement can you find in 2 Corinthians 4:17-18? How does this affect your prayer life?_____

_____

_____

CHAPTER 10
HOW SHOULD WE PRAY?

Answer me when I call to you,

O my righteous God.

Give me relief from my distress;

be merciful to me and hear my prayer...

Know that the LORD has set apart the godly for

himself; the LORD will hear when I call to him.

Psalm 4:1, 3 NIV

The Lord hears us when we call on Him and as servants of Christ, our first priority in prayer is the salvation of mankind, followed by "travail in birth again until Christ be formed in (them)"[1] bringing deliverance and full maturity.

The Holy Spirit helps us work out the salvation of our souls so that we can offer salvation to others. God sent Jesus because He loved the world. (John 3:16.) The following testimony is from St. Thérèse of Lisieux , one who gave herself to a life of prayer after a vivid spiritual vision.

> One Sunday when I was looking at a picture of Our Lord on the Cross, I saw the blood coming from one of His hands, and I felt terribly sad to think that it was falling to the earth and that no one was rushing forward to catch it. I determined to stay continually at the foot of the Cross and receive it. I knew that I should then have to spread it among other souls. The cry of Jesus on the Cross—"I am thirsty"—rang continually in my heart and set me burning with a new, intense longing. I wanted to quench the thirst of my Well-Beloved and I myself was consumed with a thirst for souls. I was concerned not with the souls of priests but with those of great sinners which I wanted to snatch from the flames of hell.[2]

Prayer prepares the pathway for a lost child or prodigal to come home. We become intercessors by the will of God according to the grace He gives and the measure of faith we receive. It is not burdensome to intercede for others when God's grace is given; on the contrary, it is a joy to know we are affecting a soul's eternal destiny.

LORD TEACH ME TO PRAY

Our four children were still stepping on my toes and sitting at the dinner table in the evenings when God came calling. From that day my life has never been the same. My starved and thirsty soul longed to know Him and read His Book. Unknown to me, the prodigal son who I gave birth to lived in my house.

Believing all was well I sat at my kitchen table or on the green couch in our living room reading my Bible aloud absorbing the meaning of each word. I remember living in the pages of the Bible; refreshing and alive—God loved me and I loved Him. In those early days I didn't realize I was a spiritual babe; I was so naive and innocent about having to work out my own salvation (a discussion for another time). I believed there was nothing that could touch my family; Jesus had suffered for us so we wouldn't have to suffer. (It would be many years before I understood any Scriptures related to suffering, such as Romans 8:17, Philippians 3:10, and 2 Timothy 2:12.) All I had to do was speak the Word and it was done!

God is so faithful, patient, and kind. After many months of reading the Bible and talking to the Father (which I didn't consider prayer at the time) I needed to learn to pray effectually. A demeaning, damaging situation came into our lives that would change the future I planned for our son. Lord, teach me to pray!

Intercessory prayer was foreign to me; it was not taught in my church, and I couldn't find anyone who could mentor me in the dynamics of this type of prayer. In fact, I was told if another person doesn't want to change I would be wasting my time praying for him. But this concerned our son, I couldn't give up; there was no one who could assure me of the results we needed concerning this situation.

The Bible was my only hope and consolation. I began looking up Scriptures concerning children, inserted our son's name in all the appropriate places, and began another stage in my prayer journey that continues today.

Praying powerful Scriptural prayers builds confidence and the more I prayed God's Word concerning children and our household, the more confidence I had God would keep His promises. I believed God had a destiny for our son, and that prayer would pave the way. I had not proven to be too hard for God, and I knew if He could deliver me from a lifetime of doom and depression, He could and would deliver our son from the snare of the enemy.

Fearlessly, confidently, and boldly I approached God with His Word. For a short time I fell into the trap of telling God how to deliver David, but the Holy Spirit was faithful to correct, lead, and guide me in my praying. He was faithful to point out the error of self-pity—the shame and remorse of having failed as a good mother—and the salvation of my wounded soul began.

Soon God's will was my will! I was in agreement with the Word of God, but I still had much to learn. Intercessory prayer became my pursuit and over the ensuing years I would learn more about this form of prayer. Little did I realize the controversy I would encounter.

RETURNING TO MY
SPIRITUAL ROOTS

My Pentecostal background (which I had left behind) had prepared the way for me to believe I could be baptized in the Holy Spirit and I could speak in a spiritual language that would bypass my emotions and psychological analyzations. I researched the Scriptures, and saw that indeed spiritual endowments (including speaking divine mysteries to the Father) are available to the believer. Not long after that our pastor took a public stand against speaking in other tongues, saying that it wasn't for today. (Speaking in other tongues is not theology or a doctrine with me, but a lifeline to the heart of the Father.)

I am deeply indebted to this pastor today for His systematic teaching of the Scriptures, but he believed "speaking in tongues" had passed away. I, however, was learning the power and effectiveness of praying divine secrets, speaking directly to the Father of spirits from my spirit. I was returning to the roots of my third generation Pentecostal background. In church I submitted to the authority God had placed there, but at home in my private devotion I was learning, growing, and developing a prayer life that would not only bring transformation to me but also to my family and others.

My purpose in sharing these personal experiences is from a heart-cry for understanding that will promote unity in the Body of Christ, between Pentecostal and Non-Pentecostal, between

Catholics and Protestants. As followers of Jesus, let us come together fulfilling the Lord's Prayer of John 17. Forgive us and past generations, O God, for those times we've used "speaking in other tongues" as a tool for division. Let's leave off the judging and condemnation; let's pursue peace, let's go after peace and let it begin with me.

> For as in one physical body we have many parts (organs, members) and all of these parts do not have the same function or use, So we, numerous as we are, are one body in Christ (the Messiah) and individually we are parts one of another [mutually dependent on one another].
>
> Romans 12:4-5 AMP

Concerning spiritual gifts, I believe as long as we are here on earth, we need spiritual endowments functioning in our lives. Whether we speak in other tongues or not, let us look to the Word of the Living God as our foundation.

INTERCESSION IN ACTION

What is intercession? It involves the lifting up in prayer of another person and is manifested in various forms. However, whatever form it may take, it is imperative our intercession places us in agreement with God's purpose...His divine order...His will. Jesus taught us to pray, "Thy kingdom come, Thy will be done in earth, as it is in heaven" (Matthew 6:10). We establish this agreement with the Lord by articulating His Word.

Through the words of the Apostle Paul, our Father has given instruction for the different kinds of prayer that will assure us a quiet and peaceable life, which is His will for us:

I exhort therefore, that, first of all, supplications, prayers, intercessions, and giving of thanks, be made for all men;

For kings, and for all that are in authority; that we may lead a quiet and peaceable life in all godliness and honesty.

1 Timothy 2:1-2

Here we see that having a good government is the will of God so we can be free to share the Gospel. As followers of Jesus we are to involve ourselves in the affairs of God and man through supplication and intercession. In the name of Jesus, we come boldly before the throne of grace, approaching God in faith and confidence, addressing Him in familiar but respectful conversational language, asking for His will to be done on earth as it is in heaven.

In order to converse with God effectively, we must learn to speak as He speaks, because the Scripture says if we ask anything according to His will, He hears us. (1 John 5:14-15.) To know God's will, study and know His written Word. His will is revealed to us in His Word—so His will is His Word.

Our confidence toward God is strong when we know what He says about the situations for which we are praying. He has given us the mind of Christ.[3] He has also provided us with His written Word so His mind can be developed within us as we study and meditate upon the Scriptures.

PRAYING IN THE SPIRIT

It was on a beautiful fall Wednesday morning when a brave, young lady came to our prayer group at Word Ministries. I invited her to have a seat, but before she sat down she announced, "You need to know that I do not speak in other tongues."

"Praying in the Spirit is not a criterion for joining us. If Jesus is your Lord and you pray in His name you are already one of us, and we welcome you here with open arms. In our prayer groups we pray with the Spirit and we pray with the understanding," I responded. Taking a deep breath she sat down, and became a vital team player or pray-er.

Even though praying in the Spirit has been a pivotal moment in the lives of many believers, there are others who have never desired this spiritual endowment (gift). My pivotal point was the discovery that God's Word is alive, that His promises are "yes" and "amen" in Christ.[4]

The temptation of many beginners is to insist everyone have the same spiritual experience. Usually it is because they have discovered great benefits and are sure that everyone would submit to this new-found spiritual exercise if they only knew about it. Zeal often gets in the way of walking in the love of God, and we try to coerce others into doing it our way. Love recognizes differences and appreciates each other's gifts as Paul tells us in the book of Romans:

> For I say, through the grace given unto me, to every man that is among you, not to think of himself more highly than he ought to think; but to think soberly, according as God hath dealt to every man the measure of faith. For as we have many members in one body, and all members have not the same office: So we, being many, are one body in Christ, and every one members one of another.
>
> Romans 12:3-5

Love chooses to walk away without criticism. Love submits to the guidelines of the group leader. Love does not compromise principles of faith even when following the guidelines of a particular prayer group. "…love does not envy; love does not parade itself, is not puffed up; does not behave rudely, does not seek its own, is not provoked, thinks no evil; does not rejoice in iniquity, but rejoices in the truth" (1 Corinthians 13:4-6 NKJV). Love seeks to keep the bond of unity and peace.

> Eagerly pursue and seek to acquire [this] love [make it your aim, your great quest]; and earnestly desire and cultivate the spiritual endowments (gifts), especially that you may prophesy (interpret the divine will and purpose

in inspired preaching and teaching). For one who speaks in an [unknown] tongue speaks not to men but to God, for no one understands or catches his meaning, because in the [Holy] Spirit he utters secret truths and hidden things [not obvious to the understanding].

1 Corinthians 14:1-2 AMP

In our town we have community prayer. We agree Jesus is Lord, and the Bible is the Word of God; we are followers of Jesus. Rather than praying our doctrines, we pray for God's will to be done. Some question whether Pentecostals and Non-Pentecostals, Catholics and Protestants can come together in harmony and unity. I believe we can when we respect and esteem one another. In John 13:34-35 Jesus gives us a new commandment: "I give you a new commandment: that you should love one another. Just as I have loved you, so you too should love one another. By this shall all [men] know that you are My disciples, if you love one another [if you keep on showing love among yourselves]" (AMP).

We need one another. Jesus prayed that we would be one even as He and the Father are one. Let us make room for one another's doctrine on this subject and not permit it to be a divisive tool of the enemy. There's a place and time for all things. God never intended for His gifts to cause confusion. When we wait on the Lord, He will show us how to pray in every situation. In Romans 8:26-27 NKJV we read:

Likewise, the Spirit also helps in our weaknesses. For we know not what we should pray for as we ought, but the Spirit Himself makes intercession for us with groanings which cannot be uttered. Now He who searches the hearts knows what the mind of Spirit is, because he makes intercession for the saints according to the will of God.

When you have exhausted your conscious knowledge of how to pray about a situation, there is still Someone who knows every aspect of the case. He also knows the mind of the Father in a way that is far above and beyond your natural understanding. Learning to wait upon the Lord has required me to get my mind quiet, and for me praying in others tongues is a spiritual weapon I use to displace distractions...submitting my thoughts to the mind of Christ.

I can say with the Apostle Paul that I speak in tongues, maybe more than you all, but in a gathering of believers I would rather pray with my understanding.

ALONE IN THE SCHOOL
OF THE SPIRIT

Let me share with you an experience I believe is an illustration of a "deeper level" of intercession.

One day, alone in my den, I began to pray for a certain minister saying, "Father, I don't know how to pray for this child of God. I have believed his latter days would be greater than before. But I don't know how to pray for him. All I know to do is pray in the Spirit because He knows Your plans." Then, after a short time of praying in the Spirit, I was aware the Spirit of God was helping me to pray. I was uttering heart-rending sobs in a language I had never expressed before in prayer.

After an interval of time, I began to pray in my natural language (English). As I listened, I found myself saying (again by the Spirit of God,) "Father, I thank You that this man is not ready to be offered up, that his time of departure is not at hand, that it is only after the fulfillment of all prophecies that he will say, 'I have fought a good fight, I have finished my course, I have kept the faith.' Then, Father, he will receive the crown of righteousness which You have laid up for him on that day."

The praying was finished and a deep peace encompassed my being. It was time for thanksgiving and praise; I began to rejoice in God my Redeemer. Later, I found out this minister believed he was finished, that no one wanted to hear what he had to say, that there was no longer a place for him in the Body of Christ.

Only the Spirit of God could have known these things. It was the Holy Spirit who was searching out the heart of this individual and who also knew the plan of God for him. While the enemy was working against him with thoughts contrary to the will of God, the Spirit of the Lord was working on His behalf through someone who responded to the call to pray. The strategy of the enemy was exposed and thwarted.

LEARNING ABOUT TRAVAIL

Another controversial form of intercession is travail, and it was my Baptist Sunday School teacher who gave me understanding on this subject. Even though some people do not believe that travail is necessary, in his letter to the Galatians, Paul opens with these words: "My little children, of whom I travail in birth again until Christ be formed in you" (Galatians 4:19). Here Paul intimates he had previously travailed for their spiritual birth, and is now travailing once again for their spiritual development and maturity.

Let's take time to explore this passage of Scripture. The Greek word translated "travail" in this verse is *odino*, a verb meaning, "to feel the pains of child birth, travail."[5] In this context, travail is a spiritual activity. Its purpose is to "bring forth" or to "give birth." As in natural childbirth, we cannot will spiritual travail to take place, nor can we "work it up," as many have tried to do; travail is not a product of the mind, will, or emotions.

The prophet Isaiah foretold of the coming Messiah: "He [God] shall see the travail of his [Jesus'] soul, and shall be satisfied" (Isaiah 53:11, parentheses mine). Jesus was the Intercessor whom God required to suffer the birth pains of redemption for all mankind. God had searched everywhere for a human intercessor and could not find one, so He assumed the responsibility Himself in the form of His Son.

Scripturally, travail has not passed away, for men will not be saved unless someone on earth prays. Through the means of prayer,

God delivers them out of the authority of darkness and translates them into the Kingdom of God's dear Son. (Colossians 1:13.) Right now, Jesus is seated at the right hand of God the Father in heaven, interceding for man. This intercession is released into the earth through His body, just as spiritual endowments are released through believers as the Spirit wills.

TRAVAIL IN THE CHURCH

Travail is often debated among the churches. My viewpoint is this: Let those who travail, travail, and let those who don't, don't. Let's not allow the Church of Jesus Christ to be divided over this issue.

This form of prayer is usually released with groanings and moanings too deep to be uttered in articulate speech. (Romans 8:26.) Travail is of the spirit, from the Holy Spirit, and not of the flesh (human nature). However, the flesh (the human mind, will, and emotions) can be affected according to an individual's interpretation of the travail process or to his or her level of spiritual understanding and maturity.

Privately (or in group prayer in which each intercessor has knowledge and understanding of travail), an individual is free to respond physically and emotionally to the workings of the Holy Spirit by yielding to Him their entire being—spirit, soul, and body. However, in public we show our respect for others by exercising extreme self-control in this area.

We govern, or hold in check, our human emotions and physical responses. The mistake that has been made in the past is: those who have placed their confidence in physical or emotional manifestations have attempted to *initiate* a work of the Spirit by crying, screaming, shaking, or moaning. Those I have interviewed say they cannot stop this physical or emotional activity. They believe they are submitted to a spiritual force greater than themselves and their behavior is beyond their control.

In 1 Corinthians 14:32 the Apostle Paul reminds us the spirit of a prophet is subject to the prophet. I believe the spirit of the intercessor is subject to the intercessor. *The Holy Spirit does not "overpower" anyone against his will, nor does He work in a manner to call undue attention to any person or group of people.* His job is to glorify Jesus Christ.

When we read the Gospels we realize there are times Jesus acts in ways that we might consider odd. Writing on the ground with His finger (John 8:6-7), or making mud with His saliva and spreading it on a man's eyes (John 9:6). We can't rule out the move of the Spirit on certain individuals that may look strange to us, but we can ask, "What is the fruit of this behavior? Is this behavior drawing people to Jesus?"

Travail is a cry before the Father and is done in the prayer closet or with those who have understanding in the area of intercession. Travail emanates from the spirit of man at the impulse of the Holy Spirit; it cannot be "worked up!" In general public worship, you should exercise the self-control that has been given to you by God the Father. (2 Timothy 1:7.)

I have experienced and observed travail in desperate circumstances. One night as I was praying with a friend, she began to travail with a fervor that could not be expressed except in cries and moans. I will attempt to describe this scene as experienced.

As my friend travailed, I prayed in the Spirit because I didn't know how to pray in this situation. The Holy Spirit revealed to us the identity of the couple for whom we were praying, and the fact that they were in a life or death situation. After a short period of time, my prayer partner was released from the travail, and the peace of God that passes understanding consumed each of us[6]— spirit, soul, and body. This peace ushered us into the rest of God. Deliverance had been brought forth and completed. (Hebrews 4:11.)

Later, we learned on that very day the husband had acquired a pistol for the purpose of killing his wife and himself. Satan's plan was thwarted when two people responded to the call to pray, and deliverance was birthed for those who did not know how to go to God for themselves. The call to prayer was released in the hearts of believers who responded to the love of God.

If you are searching for your ministry, begin here–by giving yourself to others through intercessory prayer. Let's not allow the art of intercession to be lost, or stolen from us, through ignorance and neglect. In His Word, God tells us that He will not allow our foot to be caught in a trap or hidden snare. (Proverbs 3:26.) His light will dispel the darkness if we are willing to learn from one another. Many hurts and costly mistakes can be avoided if we heed the counsel and advice of those who have walked this way before.

Let's learn to "pray one for another," as our Lord has instructed and as the Spirit leads; He always knows what is needed to bring about the desired results. (James 5:16.)

HOW THEN SHALL WE PRAY?

In 1 Timothy the Apostle Paul gives us the order of our prayer priorities:

First of all, then, I admonish and urge that petitions, prayers, intercessions, and thanksgivings be offered on behalf of all men, for kings and all who are in positions of authority or high responsibility, that [outwardly] we may pass a quiet and undisturbed life [and inwardly] a peaceable one in all godliness and reverence and seriousness in every way. For such [praying] is good and right, and [it is] pleasing and acceptable to God our Savior, Who wishes all men to be saved and [increasingly] to perceive and recognize and discern and know precisely and correctly the [divine] Truth.

2:1-4 AMP

In Ephesians 6:18 Paul says: "Pray at all times (on every occasion, in every season) in the Spirit, with all [manner of] prayer and entreaty. To that end keep alert and watch with strong purpose and perseverance, interceding in behalf of all the saints (God's consecrated people)" (AMP).

From these two references we understand we are to pray for all men and pray on every occasion with all manner of prayer and entreaty. We are to remain both mentally and spiritually alert and watch, not only in the spirit, but also the events taking place in our world. All things are parallel, and we must be a people who discern the times in which we are living. Prayer is the tool we have been given to cause change in personal and global circumstances.

Be alert! A blanket of spiritual darkness is spreading across our land and our nations are in trouble – not because of a political party but because our culture has changed. We need a spiritual reformation. It is time to reclaim our society for the Kingdom of God. This will take the involvement of leaders in all strata of society who are not afraid to speak truly, live truly, and deal truly.

Kerby Anderson, the president of Probe Ministries International, wrote in his article *The Decline of a Nation*, "Today we live in a world where biblical absolutes are ignored, and unless we return to these biblical truths, our nation will continue to decline."[7]

Will you hear the voice of God who is calling out to His children saying: "If My people, who are called by My name, shall humble themselves, pray, seek, crave, and require of necessity My face and turn from their wicked ways, then will I hear from heaven, forgive their sin, and heal their land."[8]

Are we taking this Scripture in 2 Chronicles 7:14 seriously? Are we willing to humble ourselves, pray, see, crave and require the face of God; are we willing to turn from our evil ways? How many of us have become so well-adjusted to our culture that we fit into it without even thinking? These are hard questions, but as you seek the face of God, He will reveal if you need to make adjustments in your life. Be willing to imitate Him as a child imitates his father. Allow the Bible to be your final answer to walk uprightly in all the affairs of life. As followers of Jesus let us watch our steps, use our heads, and make the most of every chance we have. Don't live carelessly, unthinkingly. Make sure you understand what the Master wants: "So watch your step. Use your head. Make the most of every chance you get. These are desperate times!" (Ephesians 5:11 MSG).

"The foundations of our society and our government rest so much on the teachings of the Bible that it would be difficult to support them if faith in these teachings would cease to be practically universal in our country."

—Calvin Coolidge, 30th President of the United States of America

PRAYER IS VITAL

In his book, *Prayer, Does it Make Any Difference?*, Philip Yancey writes:

In a scene recorded in the book of Revelation the apostle John foresees a direct linkage between the visible and invisible worlds. As a climactic moment in history, heaven is quiet. Seven angels stand with seven trumpets, waiting, for about the space of half an hour. Silence reigns, as if all heaven is listening on tiptoe. And then an angel collects the prayers of God's people on earth—all the accumulated prayers of outrage, praise, lament, abandonment, despair, petition—mixes them with incense, and presents them before the throne of God. The silence finally breaks when the fragrant prayers are hurled down to the earth: "and there came peals of thunder, rumblings, flashes of lightning and an earthquake."

"The message is clear," comments Walter Wink about that scene, "history belongs to the intercessors, who believe the future into being."[9]

The pray-ers are essential agents in the final victory over evil, suffering, and death.

The Apostle Paul admonished us to pray for our leaders. The following prayer was originally written for the government of the United States of America, but if you are from another nation, you can still use these Scriptures—just change out the words that apply.

PRAYERS THAT AVAIL MUCH®

AMERICAN GOVERNMENT

Father, in Jesus' name, we give thanks for the United States and its government. We hold up in prayer before You the men and women who are in positions of authority. We pray and intercede for the president, the representatives, the senators, the judges of our land, the policemen and the policewomen, as well as the governors and mayors, and for all those who are in authority over us in any way. We pray that the Spirit of the Lord rests upon them.

We believe that skillful and godly wisdom has entered into the heart of our president and knowledge is pleasant to him. Discretion watches over him; understanding keeps him and delivers him from the way of evil and from evil men.

Father, we ask that You compass the president about with men and women who make their hearts and ears attentive to godly counsel and do that which is right in Your sight. We believe You cause them to be men and women of integrity who are obedient concerning us that we may lead a quiet and peaceable life in all godliness and honesty. We pray that the upright shall dwell in our government—that men and women blameless and complete in Your sight, Father, shall remain in these positions of authority, but the wicked shall be cut off from our government and the treacherous shall be rooted out of it.

Your Word declares that "blessed in the nation whose God is the Lord" (Psalm 33:12). We receive Your blessing. Father, You are our Refuge and Stronghold in times of trouble (high cost, destitution, and desperation). So we declare with our mouths that Your people dwell safely in this land, and we prosper abundantly. We are more than conquerors through Christ Jesus!

It is written in Your Word that the heart of the king is in the hand of the Lord and that You turn it whichever way You desire. We believe the heart of our leader is in Your hand and that his decisions are divinely directed of the Lord.

We give thanks unto You that the good news of the Gospel is published in our land. The Word of the Lord prevails and grows mightily in the hearts and lives of the people. We give thanks for this land and the leaders You have given to us, in Jesus' name.

SCRIPTURE REFERENCES

1 Timothy 2:1-3; Proverbs 2:10-12, 21, 22; Psalm 33:12, Psalm 9:9; Deuteronomy 28:10-11; Romans 8:37 AMP; Proverbs 21:1; Acts 12:24

ANSWER THE CALL

1. In Romans 12: 4-5 AMP, the Apostle Paul tells us about the Body of Christ, specifically that we are "mutually dependent upon one another." Considering that many Christians believe Scriptures differently, how can we still be mutually dependent? _____

_____

2. According to 1 John 5:14-15, what is our guarantee that God hears our prayers?_____

_____

_____

3. In 1 Corinthians 13:4-6, we find a list of things love does and does not do. Is it possible to measure up to this? If so, how?__

_____

_____

4. If we are with a group of diverse believers, is it appropriate to speak out a message in tongues or travail in prayer? Why? (Read 2 Timothy 1:7.)_____

_____

_____

5. According to Ephesians 6:18 how are we to pray?_____

_____

_____

CHAPTER 11
GODLY WISDOM
FOR INTERCESSION

If any of you lacks wisdom, let him ask of God, who gives to all liberally and without reproach, and it will be given to him.

But let him ask in faith, with no doubting, for he who doubts is like a wave of the sea driven and tossed by the wind.

James 1:5-6 NKJV

B elieving that I had heard from God I approached the pastor about leading a prayer group that would meet before the evening service. This was not to be. Even though I explained I would teach those who came how to interact with the church leadership according to the royal law of love and godly wisdom, she refused the offer. I listened as she explained that previous intercessors came to her after each service to let her know

God had shown them exactly what would happen, even the message she would bring. The intercessors thought the pastor would recognize they were being led by the Holy Spirit, instead believing they were trying to control her, she demanded they quit meeting. Out of her past experiences and pain she encouraged the members to look to her rather than the Holy Spirit, and she began controlling what they prayed and how they prayed. This pastor carried a heavy load believing she was anointed to hear from God for each of her church members. If Jesus needed the support of his friends, how much more do we need others to pray for us in agreement with the will of God?

Prayer is a vital pillar in any church. Without prayer, a church is in danger of becoming a social organization, failing to meet the spiritual needs of the congregation. Even though the Word of God may be taught, without prayer it becomes a legalistic form, void of power. Today, our world is in turmoil and needs a spiritual reformation—the Church needs revival. Think of what could happen if the Church obeyed the one commandment Jesus gave us. We are to love one another as He has loved us. (John 13:34.) What might happen if God's people prayed, not their own agendas, but according to His will?

Prayer is essential. It is also of utmost importance that those who desire to pray be taught, guided, and instructed in the art of intercession—in love and with wisdom by those who understand intercessory prayer. One of Satan's plans for the destruction of the

Church is to remove from the Body of Christ effective prayer. His tactics include keeping us busy with one program after another. It is easy to neglect our prayer time when we get caught up with the activities of the church world.

THE PENTECOSTAL AWAKENING

Historically, there has been much prayer before every great revival. The fires of revival often have "wildfire" close by. It seems with every move of God there are extremes, fanaticism, and even abuses of the "new" revelation. In his book, *Like a Mighty Army*, Charles W. Conn writes about the history of the Church of God denomination which has its roots in a revival known as "The Pentecostal Awakening."[1] My paternal grandmother, a widow who depended on God for wisdom to run the family farm, became a part of this great revival.

Later my dad, the late Rev. A. H. "Buck" Griffin, was ordained as a Bishop in the Church of God. When I asked my parents for prayer instruction my mother, Donnis Brock Griffin, talked about her intimate relationship with the Holy Spirit. My dad encouraged me to study the Scriptures and allow the Bible to be my authority in prayer. He, also, shared some of the early mistakes made by people who loved God, but were drawn away by false teachings.

Charles W. Conn writes, "Every revival period has had to combat a frightful and ever-present siege of fanaticism and superstition, which has alterably assumed a form in keeping with the type of revival accomplished and peculiar to the times and circumstances of its appearance."[2]

I am thankful for the faithful who exercised wisdom, remained teachable, and wanted only to do the will of God. They were students of the Bible—men and women of prayer who remained well-balanced, walking in communion with the Holy Spirit. They became known for their belief and practice of *glossolalia*[3] (a Latin word for "tongue"), an experience of the early church on the day of Pentecost.

And they were all filled with the Holy Spirit and began to speak in other tongues, as the Spirit gave them utterance.

Acts 2:4 NKJV

During the early days of the Pentecostal movement in our country, fanaticism and abuse of the gifts of the Holy Spirit on the part of some people caused many other followers of Jesus to reject the experience known as the Baptism in the Holy Spirit with the evidence of speaking in tongues.

In my generation, although we talked about the Holy Spirit and speaking in tongues, I dare say the average churchgoer had no concept of the proper usage and purpose of tongues. It was my understanding the Holy Spirit was some kind of mystical "force" which mysteriously came upon people, overpowering them with

His presence and causing them to do all kinds of strange and unreasonable things. (This misconception was later corrected as the ministers began to teach the doctrine, person, and nature of the Holy Spirit.)

Messages in tongues were given without any interpretation, often at inopportune or inappropriate times, interrupting the service. Unfortunately, many became more enthralled with the gifts than with the Giver of the gifts.

My dad told me about being in prayer groups where red hot coals from the fireplace were passed around from hand to hand as some kind of spiritual ritual. In the church meetings burning oil or kerosene lamps were taken to individuals. An unseen force seemingly caused them to pass their hands through the open flames, or they grasped the globe with both hands. The act itself was done to prove that the power of God was present and would prevent damage to the body. To them it symbolized Isaiah 43:2, "…when thou walkest through the fire, thou shalt not be burned; neither shall the flame kindle upon thee." This practice is not scriptural. Jesus says in Matthew 4:7, "You shall not tempt the LORD your God" (NKJV). God's mercy and grace must have protected some in their ignorance, but it was certainly not His will.

A few actually believed this was the power of God moving, but many were repelled by these and other bizarre actions, even though they saw the protection of God in these situations. At one time in that society, when a person spoke in tongues, he was thought to have achieved the ultimate in spiritual maturity. A few false ministers taught it was impossible for one sealed with the Holy Spirit to ever sin again.

In spite of these abuses there were many who received this gift of grace and were strengthened, brought to new levels of spiritual maturity, had a love for the Word of God and served the Lord with joyful hearts. The Spirit of God in them proved to be greater than the fanaticism and false teachings. The "Pentecostal Revival" survived, and several dynamic Pentecostal denominations have become known around the world.

THE CHARISMATIC RENEWAL

Several years later, a revival known as the Charismatic Renewal attracted many from major denominations. They experienced a supernatural move of the Holy Spirit and they began to gather for worship and praise. Men and women received the Baptism in the Holy Spirit and began speaking in strange languages, which they referred to as their prayer language. Unbelievers who came either out of curiosity or looking for help experienced salvation and the Baptism of the Holy Spirit.

Lives were changed and a desire to see others delivered from bondages opened the door for prayer groups to be formed. Wives and husbands wanted their unsaved spouses to accept this phenomenal experience, and prayer groups were formed to bring them and other family members into the new "fold." But again "wildfire" flamed on the periphery of the real move of God. It wasn't long before prayer groups formed and bizarre activities occurred causing many to run from prayer groups.

Before long, pastors were shying away from anyone who was identified as an "intercessor." Inexperienced, self-appointed leaders whose ministries appeared to outgrow their spiritual development hurt many new believers. Demonstrations of the "anointing" became more important than godly character and immorality was tolerated in some groups. God's grace was abused, and the Body of Christ suffered as their spiritual heroes fell from their pedestals. However, in spite of disappointments and hurts, those who had come into a relationship with the Father-God remained faithful and true to the Scriptures.

It seemed the renewed interest in prayer would be toppled before it began. Satan was on the attack! Paul writes in 2 Corinthians 2:11 "…we are not ignorant of his (Satan's) devices." At one time "spiritual warfare" became the rage of many in the Body of Christ. My husband and I attended a spiritual warfare retreat where we were told if the level of noise hurt our ears, we had demons and would need to be delivered. Strange manifestations and sounds came forth, but we could find no scriptural support for these activities. A lot of attention was given to the devil!

Rick Renner counsels in his book, *Dressed to Kill*, "If spiritual warfare is not taught properly, it can be devastating, for this subject has a unique way of captivating people's attention so completely that they eventually think of nothing but spiritual warfare. This is a favorite trick of the devil to make believers magnify his power to a greater degree than it deserves." [4]

The Spirit of Truth uses Scripture to teach spiritual things. It seems down through the history of the Church, God preserved a remnant of people who would seek Him, wait on Him and pray for His will to be done on earth even as it is in heaven. 2 Timothy 3:16-17 NKJV says, "All Scripture is given by inspiration of God, and is profitable for doctrine, for reproof, for correction, for instruction in righteousness, that the man of God may be complete, thoroughly equipped for every good work."

Thank God for what the Charismatic revival taught us. This movement has spilled over into interdenominational church fellowships. While some thrive, others become more and more legalistic, dogmatic, and controlled by man. Well-balanced prayer ministries survived the attacks of the enemy. God brought together those who would submit to godly wisdom and instruction. We have to remain teachable! Let us be spiritually alert and pray with purpose.

INTERCESSION TODAY

I know today that to accomplish the work of the Lord we need the prayerful aid and support of others. The cooperation of both leadership and laymen is required. The key to purposeful and powerful ministry is prayer—praying prayers that avail much.

Intercessory prayer groups are needed, and I believe that they can be very beneficial where the pastors and leadership are men and women of prayer. In my opinion, every church needs a Pastor of Prayer or an Elder/Deacon of Prayer on staff. Prayer is vital to the spiritual success and life of a church and community.

It is necessary for a ministry leader to maintain close contact with the prayer group for the purpose of remaining in unity. A group led by the pastor himself has direct counsel and knowledge of the specific areas of concern in the church.

A mistake made by some ministers is depending solely on the "intercessor" to hear from God for the direction of the ministry. When this happens, the responsibility for church guidance has been shifted from the pastor to the intercessor. In that case, the intercessor is placed in a position to exercise control over a ministry in a very subtle manner. If that control is allowed to continue, the results can be detrimental to both the ministry and the intercessor. Team members are not to make decisions apart from the leadership or try to control ministry decisions. If an intercessor accepts the responsibility of hearing from God for a church or other ministry—whether that responsibility is self-imposed or delegated by the pastor—a door is opened for pride to enter the heart of the intercessor.

In the Amplified Bible, pride is described as, "A proud look [the spirit that makes one overestimate himself and underestimate others]" (Proverbs 6:17). There is an established line of authority in the Church, and when it is violated for prideful reasons, Satan (who is a shrewd legalist), takes advantage of the situation. There are people who desire a position of authority in their church or ministry, but few are prepared or equipped to handle the heavy burden of responsibility that goes with authority. A pastor or ministry leader must never relinquish to another his God-given privilege, responsibility of spiritual leadership, and determination of God's direction for the church.

No member of a prayer group is to attempt to assume the responsibility of the pastor, as happened in a certain local church. (This pastor gave me permission to share about this incident.) The intercessors began receiving "insight" about other members of the church, and demanded the pastor turn certain persons out of the church. (These intercessors happened to be good people who loved the Lord and truly wanted to work for Him.) But when the pastor wisely refused to comply with their demands, they refused to listen to their pastor.

The conclusion of the affair was the intercessors ended up moving their membership to another church, still convinced that they were right. They sincerely believed since they had "heard from God" in the matter, the pastor was obviously in disobedience to God's will and purpose.

Always remain teachable, and ask God to give you the grace to resist a dictatorial and overbearing attitude. The constant ministry of transformation is available. Resist the deadly sin of pride.

When I talked with these ladies who loved God, I recognized they wanted to grow in knowledge and wisdom. God did great things in their lives and they became productive members in the Body of Christ. They explained to me that they thought they were operating in the "discerning of spirits." But the day came when they heard and received sound, well-balanced teaching on the gifts of the Spirit.

DISCERNING OF SPIRITS

Discerning of spirits is referred to in 1 Corinthians 12. This "gift" operates as the Spirit of God wills; it never becomes the personal "possession" or prerogative of the individual through whom it operates. In the situation with the ladies of the church, deception had given way to a critical and judgmental spirit. In his book, *Questions and Answers on Spiritual Gifts*, Howard Carter points out:

There are those who have, perhaps unconsciously, criticized their brethren, and have believed they were manifesting this gift [the discerning of spirits] when they supposedly detected 'demon power' in nearly every meeting they have entered. They profess to see demon power in the services, demon influences moving the speaker, demon spirits everywhere. They have accounted for every lack of blessing by demon power only, and they have seen nothing by their supposed exercise of the gift but what has been bad...."[5]

True intercessory prayer adheres to Scripture. Constantly looking for problems and inadequacies in every situation leads to operating in negativism instead of in the power of the Holy Spirit. It may be ego-building to suppose you know the faults of others through the so-called "discerning of spirits," but the intercessor is to be continually clothed in humility.

The purpose of the gift of the discerning of spirits is "to recognize the presence of Satan in an individual's life to deliver him from Satan's grasp and to glorify Christ. The gift of discerning of spirits also includes the discerning of angelic spirits. God has made angels ministering spirits; many times people discern that an angel is near."[6]

There was a time when I prayed at the top of my voice because I heard someone say that the devil is hard of hearing. I screamed "binding and loosening" prayers feeling powerful. I'm so thankful for the Holy Spirit who is our Teacher. Patiently, He waited for me to ask Him to teach me how to apply the prayers of binding and loosening. He was so faithful to bring the teaching I asked for. Intercession is collaboration between you and the Holy Spirit.

My Personal Struggle

On one leg of my journey, I served as pastor of a church. I was convinced even after the honeymoon was over prayer would see us through, and prayer kept me and those who stood beside me during the fallout. (Actually, prayer kept those who were in opposition to what I believe was God's will for that time.) Later, I would realize prayer *prepares* one for good communication, but it was never intended to *replace* good communication. I waited for God's plan to unfold while I continued to seek Him. I lived in Psalm 27, especially verse four:

One thing have I asked of the Lord, that will I seek, inquire for, and [insistently] require: that I may dwell in the house of the Lord [in His presence] all the days of my life, to behold and gaze upon the beauty [the sweet attractiveness and the delightful loveliness] of the Lord and to meditate, consider, and inquire in His temple (AMP).

God by His grace kept me strong in the Lord and the power of His might as the storm raged around me. Even those whom I had taught for several years and most of my staff aligned themselves against me; new members decided I was in sinful disobedience. (Their "authority" told them God never calls a woman to pastor.) They said they opposed me because they loved me, and I believe, even today, they were sincere in that belief.

After implementing the plan God gave us for the church, I resigned and withdrew from everyone except my family and a few friends who had stood with me. The prayer and teaching ministry, known as Word Ministries, Inc., continued.

Before I recovered from the storm, our son who had walked free from addictions for six years, went back into his lifestyle of addiction. (In his testimony he shares how "religion" became his addiction during those six years.) Over time he became a stranger to us. The few times he would come to family gatherings, we waltzed all around the "big gray elephant" that was taking up space in our family. The Holy Spirit taught me how to let go and let God, and I rested from the spiritual warfare. For a period of time, I didn't pray. However, I continued researching Scripture and writing prayers for others to pray.

My prayer life took on a new tone and I was enjoying my time apart from the "church-world." Most of my prayer time was spent in silence, receiving the unconditional love of the Father while basking in His arms of mercy. When the time came for me to go back to the mainland at the instruction of the Holy Spirit, I balked because I didn't think I would ever learn to trust church people again.

A Desert Place

Word Ministries continued. I traveled, speaking at churches and prayer retreats. Then, after the deliverance of our son from a lifestyle of addiction, my prayer life became a desert place. Reading the Bible was laborious; praying was akin to treading water wondering when "help" might come. I grew weary but knew there was nowhere else to go. If God was speaking, I couldn't hear Him. Counting it all joy was a chore, and it seemed God was distancing Himself from me. My cries for help went unanswered, except for brief moments. But I convinced my mind that "Standing Somewhere in the Shadows"[7] I would find the Captain of my Salvation.

My most memorable times of prayer during this dry period were praying with the team members of the *Prayers That Avail Much®* prayer groups. Every time we met for prayer was special. There were visitations from God and I would leave refreshed and knowing that breakthrough had come, only to return to a desert place once again. Today I refer to this time as the "dark night of my soul."

My library increased as I purchased more books and tapes on emotional healing, prayer, and meditation. I listened to Norman Vincent Peale and read books on emotional healing—books by Brennan Manning, Madam Guyon, Saint Teresa of Avila, Saint John of the Cross, Saint Augustine, Thomas Merton, and many others who offered their bodies as living sacrifices on the altar of prayer.

Over time I returned to my First Love. The Book of Ephesians became dearer to me than ever. I fell in love with the Lover of my soul and experienced the love of Christ which passes knowledge. "The Old Rugged Cross,"[8] a song from my childhood, became more precious than ever. I marvel that God Incarnate in the person of Jesus Christ would come to earth as a baby! He could have chosen another method, but He chose to grow up in a family...to be tempted in every way as we are. Mighty God, Glorious Father, Emmanuel—God with us!

I hope you are encouraged and renewed as you read about the prayer journey of a fellow follower of Jesus. When I make mistakes, God is faithful to forgive me and teach me Truth; He shows me the way to walk. I learned not to lean on my own understanding. Today, in all my ways I acknowledge Him and He directs the paths of my journey. (Proverbs 3:5-6.)

The Father is glorified as we experience answered prayer; witness the deliverance and salvation of children and loved ones, the healing of family and marriage relationships. Today, testimonies continue to pour into the ministry from others whose prayer lives have been changed as they learned to pray *Prayers That Avail Much®*. I've witnessed the spiritual growth and emotional healing of those who attend the Bible studies. Nothing thrills my heart more than seeing eyes light up with understanding and joy. This life of prayer continues to be an exciting journey.

Today my prayer time is more contemplative than before; I listen for the Voice that speaks in the quiet secret places. God by His Spirit continues to impart knowledge, understanding, and wisdom to this follower of Jesus and I am still learning about this inexhaustible subject of prayer in the School of the Spirit. The prayer of intercession continues to unfold, and if there's ever been a time that this form of prayer is needed, it is *now!*

The following prayer was written to encompass your prayer group with God's Word to ensure communication and unity.

PRAYERS THAT AVAIL MUCH®

COMMUNICATION WITH
GROUP MEMBERS

Father, to as many as received Jesus, You gave the power to become Your sons and daughters. I am learning to be straightforward in my communications with my brothers and sisters in Christ, my co-laborers in the Lord. I have the power to be direct, honestly expressing my feelings and desires, because Jesus has been made unto me wisdom. Wisdom from above is straightforward, impartial (unbiased, objective), and unfeigned (free from doubts, wavering, and insincerity.)

I am Your creation, Father, and You created me to be active in sharing my faith, so that I will have full understanding of every good thing we have in Christ. It is my prayer in Jesus' name that my conversation will always be full of grace, seasoned with salt, so that I may know how to answer everyone. I am content with my own reality (satisfied to the point where I am not disturbed or disquieted) in whatever state I am, so those around me can feel safe in my presence. I will speak truly, deal truly, and live truly, expressing the truth in love.

As Your children and co-laborers, we walk in the ever-developing maturity that enables us to be in perfect harmony and full agreement in what we say, perfectly united in our common understanding and in our opinions and judgments. And if on some point we think differently, You will make it clear to us. We live up to what we have already attained in our individual lives and in our group. We will let our yes be simply yes, and our no be simply no. In Jesus' name, amen.

Scripture References

John 1:12; 1 Corinthians 1:30; James 3:17 AMP; Philemon 6 NIV; Colossians 4:6 NIV; Philippians 4:11 AMP; Ephesians 4:15 AMP; 1 Corinthians 1:10 AMP; Philippians 3:15-17; Matthew 5:37 AMP

ANSWER THE CALL

1. In the Pentecostal Awakening believers were known for their practice of glossolalia, or the practice of "speaking in tongues" (Acts 2:4). Is it possible for those who have experienced this gift and those who have not, to come together in prayer?_____

_____

_____

2. During both the Pentecostal Awakening and the later Charismatic Renewal there were cases of fanaticism and abuse. How does a believer avoid being caught up in these extremes? (See 2 Timothy 3:16-17.)_____

_____

3. Pride is one of the most dangerous traps an intercessor or spiritual leader can get caught in. (see Proverbs 6:17 AMP.) Have you ever felt you stepped over the line in this area?

_____

_____

4. In 1 Corinthians 12:11 the Scripture says the Spirit gives spiritual to gifts to each one as He wills. What is the danger of intercessors that operate in the gift of discerning of spirits?_____

_____

_____

CHAPTER 12
PITFALLS OF INTERCESSION

For the Lord shall be your confidence, firm *and* strong, and shall keep your foot from being caught [in a trap or some hidden danger]. Withhold not good from those to whom it is due [its rightful owners], when it is in the power of your hand to do it.

Proverbs 3:26-27 AMP

In his book, *Dressed to Kill*, Rick Renner writes: "Regardless of how good the flesh looks or how loud the flesh roars, it was never intended to fight a spiritual foe."[1]

Unfortunately, agents of prayer sometimes feel the most powerful when they are being demonstrative and loudly waging war. Having been invited to a "warfare" conference, I watched as honest-hearted believers threw karate chops into the air while roaring, hissing, or barking. Using the Word of God as my guide I simply could not find any scriptural basis for these physical activities.

Let us not be ignorant of Satan's devises. In C. S. Lewis' book, *Screwtape Letters,* he points out that if the devil couldn't keep us from obeying God, he would at least devise ways to keep us off balance.[2]

LACK OF KNOWLEDGE

I bear them witness that they have a [certain] zeal and enthusiasm for God, but it is not enlightened and according to [correct and vital] knowledge.

Romans 10:2 AMP

The zeal of many Christians far exceeds their ability to rightly divide the Word of God. Zeal and enthusiasm are necessary in maintaining an effective prayer life, but intercessors become subject to the designs of the devil when they do not rightly divide the Word of God. God's Word is truth, and when an individual is seeking truth, the Father will get that truth to him. Jesus says His sheep know the voice of the Good Shepherd.[3] We cannot know His voice apart from His Word.

In my early days of searching for the truth about how to pray prayers that would avail much, I attended several different prayer groups. I learned more about what not to do than what to do.

At one church prayer meeting, a young lady, who was a new Christian, wanted the group to pray that a mountain of difficulty in her life would be removed and cast into the sea. She went on to reveal the "mountain" was her husband. So dutifully everyone in the group began to pray earnestly this young woman's husband would be "removed" and "cast into the sea!"

As she gave the account of the problem, it came to me the poor man was probably tired of sitting home alone night after night while his wife was out attending prayer meetings, church services, Bible studies, and seminars. That night he asked her to stay home with him, and according to her testimony, she informed him that he was of the devil. Understandably, a heated discussion then ensued in the home and she was still upset when she shared her grief.

Much zeal in praying about the "removal" of her "problem" was displayed in the prayer session. I wondered why there was no one to give her scriptural instruction.

Intercession is a serious business. It can either be a vital asset to a church, or a detriment to the spiritual condition and reputation of that ministry. Christians need to adhere to Paul's admonition in 1 Thessalonians 5:12: "...get to know those who labor among you [recognize them for what they are]..." (AMP).

Those who desire to be in a prayer group are encouraged to become students of the Word of God, willing to submit to the leader who relies on the written Word for guidance and confirmation. This leader, whose heart is perfect toward God, is properly submitted to the pastor and to those in authority over him or her, and to the church doctrines, before attempting to teach the Scriptures concerning how to pray effectively.

MISUSE OF SCRIPTURES

In most prayer groups, the prayer of agreement, as presented by Jesus in Matthew 18:19, is one of the most misunderstood and abused concepts in the Bible:

Again I say unto you, That if two of you shall agree on earth as touching any thing that they shall ask, it shall be done for them of my Father which is in heaven.

The Lord taught me much about this Scripture after a vivid experience in my marriage. The intercessors in the prayer group, which I had organized, agreed with me that my husband would go with me to an upcoming seminar I wanted us to attend together.

At this time Everette did not seem to be interested in the work God had called me to do. (I was seeking more and more of Jesus, and would go with friends or alone to hear various Bible teachers.) Although he refused to go with me, Everette did not hinder me from going. After a while, my desire to have my husband attend these meetings with me became a consuming fire within me. Many times when alone, I cried all the way to a service because I wanted my life's partner by my side. I tried everything! I would hear testimonies of how God was bringing couples into total harmony and agreement. I even saw it happening in the marriages of some of the ladies who were attending the Bible study I was teaching.

Everette ignored all my pleas and the devices to which I resorted in my efforts to get him to go with me. At last, I made my request to the group for prayer for my situation. I was sure my "time" had arrived because the intercessors entered into that prayer of agreement with me. There was no doubt in my mind that Everette would go. I believed the Bible! Jesus says that "anything" that we ask in agreement would be done for us of the Father. (Matthew 18:19.)

The first night of the meeting came and went. But Everette did not. He stayed at home, and I attended with friends. The second night came and went. Everette did not budge. I attended with friends. Finally, it was the third night of the meeting—God's last chance to answer our "binding" prayer of agreement. Two seats were reserved in the front row of the auditorium—one for me, and one for my husband. As the time for the service approached, I turned down all offers of a ride to the meeting because I just *knew* that my night of triumph had arrived.

It was past time to leave for the meeting and I was still waiting, sure that Everette was going. Finally, he turned to me and said, "If you are going to the service tonight, you'd better leave. You're already late."

I struggled to open my mouth in protest that he just *had* to go with me, but before I could form the words, he closed the subject: "You need to know that you and your friends cannot 'confess' me into going. My mind is made up; I am staying home to watch the World Series on television."

At the meeting I was met by an usher who walked me down that long aisle to the reserved seats while everyone's eyes followed me step by step; at least I felt them watching me. I knew God could not fail, so I was convinced we had missed God somewhere. Still, I couldn't understand where we had gone wrong. The intercessors and I had done everything we knew how to do, and on top of that, we believed. Besides, hadn't I put "corresponding action" to my faith by refusing all other rides to the meeting? I had acted in accordance with my faith, and that was *supposed* to be the measure of what I received.

There was no lack of zeal on *my* part—or that of the intercessors. But there was also no Everette at the meeting. I sought God asking for His wisdom and knowledge.

Yes, my friends and I had zeal. However, our zeal for God was not enlightened according to correct and vital knowledge. Without that knowledge, our zeal was worthless. Because of a lack of revelation knowledge, we had misused the prayer of agreement. I had taken Scripture out of context, "confessed" my own selfish desire and then expected God to act in response to my misguided "faith." He didn't do it. God does not violate His Word in order to answer an improper prayer. This prayer was all about me and my desire; not about God. I wanted to prove my faith, which was the wrong motive and I didn't want to be alone in my public walk with God.

When you are searching for truth, the spirit of error cannot prevail for long. God is patient with His people and gives the Holy

Spirit to us to instruct us. In this instance, the Spirit began to do His work of enlightenment in me. One word kept coming to my mind, a word I was increasingly sure was God's answer to my question of where we had gone wrong.

The Spirit showed me that in this case what the intercessors and I had engaged in was not spiritual intercession, but *manipulation.* Our "spiritual prayer of agreement" had actually been nothing more than an act of the flesh—one which Paul refers to in Galatians 5:20 as "witchcraft!" We had tried to control another person's actions by use of the intellect through prayer and positive confession. I realized it was not my friends' agreement I had needed in that situation—it was Everette's!

That night I released my husband's "freedom of choice" to God. I too was set free. I realized my husband was not against me, but for me. I returned to him what he had given me—the freedom to hear from God and to obey the voice of the Good Shepherd *as an individual.* The very next year another seminar was scheduled, and to my surprise Everette not only attended voluntarily, he also served as an usher by his own volition. I went with him to all the evening services.

All prayer is to be based on Scripture. If you are praying for your mate, pray according to God's Word, not according to your plans, which are often selfish, and for your own benefit. Ask the Holy Spirit to teach you how to love unconditionally and accept your spouse just as God accepted you.

My desire and prayer for Everette became: "Our Father which art in heaven, hallowed be Thy Name. Thy Kingdom come. Thy will be done in Everette's life, as it is in heaven."[4] The Holy Spirit gave me many other Scriptures of support for this prayer. God forgave me for attempting to usurp my husband's authority and free will.

The only person who never makes a mistake is the one who never does anything. Thank God "every Scripture is God-breathed (given by His inspiration) and profitable for instruction, for reproof and conviction of sin, for correction of error and discipline in obedience, [and] for training in righteousness (in holy living, in conformity to God's will in thought, purpose, and action)" (2 Timothy 3:16 AMP). When you make a mistake, ask forgiveness and receive it. Thank God for forgiveness and correction that you will become a fit vessel for the Master's use.

It is imperative that an intercessor heed sound teaching and "...be filled with the full (deep and clear) knowledge of His will in all spiritual wisdom [in comprehensive insight into the ways and purposes of God] and in understanding and discernment of spiritual things" (Colossians 1:9 AMP). The intercessor submits to the constant ministry of transformation by the Holy Spirit: "Let our lives lovingly express truth [in all things, speaking truly, dealing truly, living truly]. Enfolded in love, let us grow up in every way and in all things into Him Who is the Head, [even] Christ (the Messiah, the Anointed One)" (Ephesians 4:15 AMP). Do not neglect your study of God's Word. The Holy Spirit will guide you into *all* truth.[5]

If any of you lacks wisdom, let him ask of God, who gives to all liberally and without reproach, and it will be given to him.

But let him ask in faith, with no doubting, for he who doubts is like a wave of the sea driven and tossed by the wind.

James 1:5-6 NKJV

EMOTION VERSUS SPIRIT

Usually there is at least one member in a prayer group who is more emotional than others. For some unknown reason, people will tend to look upon this one as being very spiritual. They will begin to depend on the emotional reactions of this individual as a sign of the effectiveness of their prayers, or for evidence to determine whether the prayer has been answered or not.

For example, if he or she is crying, that is taken as a sign more intercession is needed. Laughter might mean the prayer has been heard and answered.

God does not lead us by our emotions, but by His Spirit: "For as many as are led by the Spirit of God, they are the sons of God" (Romans 8:14). His Word is a light unto our path, and a lamp unto our feet. (Psalm 119:105.) He leads us by His Word, His peace, and the inner witness: "...let the peace (soul harmony which comes) from Christ rule (act as umpire continually) in your hearts [deciding and settling with finality all questions that arise in your minds...]" (Colossians 3:15 AMP).

The writer of Hebrews asks: "...shall we not much rather be in subjection unto the Father of spirits, and live?" (Hebrews 12:9). God is a Spirit, and those who worship Him must do so "in spirit and in truth" (John 4:24). In Romans 8:14, Paul gives us insight into how we are to relate to God our Father when he points out that those who are led by the Spirit are the true sons of God. Also, in Romans 8:16 it says the Spirit Himself bears witness with our spirit that we are the children of God. It appears from these Scriptures God is the One who deals with us Spirit to spirit.

VISIONS AND VOICES

Depending on visions and voices apart from the Word of God is dangerous and will lead to spiritual experiences which are not of God. One woman who was being ministered to presented her urgent prayer request concerning two rebellious teenagers who were creating problems in her home.

The group immediately went into loud, thunderous, earnest prayer. After a while the mother fell on the floor and a young lady, who seemed to be the leader of the group, began to have a vision of a beautiful casket dripping with jewels. As she finished relating her vision, which offered no answer to the problem at hand in my opinion, everyone became very excited about the vision which had been recounted in very religious terms.

Later, I tried to share the Word of God with the lady who had the problem. She told me she wasn't interested in what the Bible had to say because she already felt better.

Do not be led astray by voices or visions! God is not "flaky" and He does not want His children acting "flaky." Somehow some people have established the idea that to be spiritual one must act weird (and sometimes we may). But acting weird does not make us spiritual. *Prayer is a spiritual business, and effective prayers are governed by spiritual laws that are placed there for our protection.* If we adhere to the status and teachings of the Bible, people will be drawn to us, not driven away from us.

FLESHLY MANIFESTATIONS

I received the most bizarre letter from an intercessory prayer group leader. She described how two women in her group were acting. When a prayer request was shared, one of the women would begin to act like a dog, getting down on her hands and knees, clawing and scratching. Her friend would then follow her around, "casting out evil spirits," while this woman clawed her legs, even to the point of drawing blood. This practice was driving people away from the group, and the leader did not know how to deal with the situation. Supposedly the one who acted like a dog took on all the evil spirits of the individual for whom the group was interceding. As her friend "cast out the evil spirits from her," it was said to bring deliverance to the person being tormented.

The pastor was unaware of what was happening in this group. I advised this leader to go to the pastor immediately and explain to him what was taking place. These activities were of the flesh (physical manifestations contrived mentally), but applied as if they were spiritually perceived and derived. Later, I received a good report from this church. God had brought them revelation knowledge on prayer through a responsible, effective seminar on intercession.

May God grant more and more revelation knowledge and may wisdom be forthcoming in the days ahead!

FAITH MIXED WITH THE WORD

One of the quickest ways to sabotage your prayers of petition, supplication, and intercession is to become confused about the will of God concerning that for which you are praying. Your faith mixed with God's Word will dispel confusion: "Wherefore also it is contained in the scripture, Behold, I lay in Sion a chief corner stone, elect, precious: and he that believeth on him shall not be confounded" (1 Peter 2:6). To be "confounded" is to be confused, and confusion is an enemy to effective intercession.

We live by the faith of the Son of God who loved us and gave Himself for us. (Galatians 2:20.) As long as the faith we exercise is based on truth, we will not become confused. There are many voices out there to distract us. Let us purpose to know the Word of God and mix faith with it, knowing the Father's voice is our surety. The Father cares for His children.

Speaking of the Lord Jesus, Peter tells us:

Unto you therefore which believe he is precious: but unto them which be disobedient, the stone which the builders disallowed, the same is made the head of the corner, And a stone of stumbling, and a rock of offence, even to them which stumble at the word, being disobedient...."

1 Peter 2:7-8

The disobedient stumble over the Word of God, usually, because they haven't yet received the revelation of the Father's great love for them. Other than the companionship and communion of the Holy Spirit, the most vital aspect involved in our triumphant stand against the enemy is the Word of God. As intercessors, it isn't enough for us just to know the Word, but we are to, also, be obedient to the Word, not stumbling over it again and again by refusing to obey it. When we live in such a manner the enemy cannot bring a charge against us.

By grace you have been saved, by grace you have been made the righteousness of God in Christ Jesus. (2 Corinthians 5:21.) It is the fervent prayers of a righteous person that avails much. (James 5:16.) We have to know we have been made the righteousness of God. Why would anyone believe this? Because the Bible tells us so. But when we enter into disobedience by refusing to obey the Word, we leave ourselves open for Satan to bring a charge against us and our confidence in God diminishes. When we follow after the Spirit, and not after the flesh, who can bring a charge against us? It is God Who justifies, Who puts us into right relation to Himself. (Romans 8:33.) God does not accuse or impeach those whom He has chosen.

When we are praying for others, it is with clean hands and a pure heart that we enforce the laws of the Spirit of Life in Christ Jesus, reaffirming the devil's defeat. Known sin in our life strips us of confidence toward God and of the assurance in His divine ability to exercise power and authority over the enemy. As for you, your part is to stay in the Word and to speak truly, deal truly, and live truly; God will help you. (Ephesians 4:15.) Bring faults before the Father and request His help. Keep your conscience clear and the enemy will not be able to drive a wedge between you and your Lord or hinder your prayers.

The following prayer lays a strong foundation for you to live your life by the Word of God.

PRAYERS THAT AVAIL MUCH®

TO WALK IN THE WORD

Father, in the name of Jesus, *I commit myself to walk in the Word.* Your Word living in me produces Your life in this world. I recognize that Your Word is integrity itself—steadfast, sure, eternal—and I trust my life to its provisions.

You have sent Your Word forth into my heart. I let it dwell in me richly in all wisdom. I meditate in it day and night so that I may diligently act on it. The Incorruptible Seed, the Living Word, the Word of Truth, is abiding in my spirit. That Seed is growing mightily in me now, producing Your nature, Your life. It is my counsel, my shield, my buckler, my powerful weapon in battle. The Word is a lamp to my feet and a light to my path. It makes my way plain before me. I do not stumble, for my steps are ordered in the Word.

The Holy Spirit leads and guides me into all truth. He gives me understanding, discernment, and comprehension so that I am preserved from the snares of the evil one.

I delight myself in You and Your Word. Because of that, You put Your desires within my heart. I commit my way unto You, and You bring it to pass. I am confident that You are at work in me now both to will and to do all Your good pleasure.

I exalt Your Word, hold it in high esteem, and give it first place. *I make my schedule around Your Word.* I make the Word the final authority to settle all questions that confront me. I choose to agree with the Word of God, and I choose to disagree with any thoughts, conditions, or circumstances contrary to Your Word. I boldly and confidently say that my heart is fixed and established on the solid foundation—the living Word of God! Amen.

SCRIPTURE REFERENCES

Romans 5:5; 1 John 2:5; 1 John 4:19; 1 Corinthians 13:4-8 AMP; Romans 12:14 AMP; Matthew 5:44; Philippians 1:9-11; John 13:34; 1 Corinthians 3:6; Daniel 1:9 AMP; Ephesians 3:17 AMP; Romans 8:31, 39

ANSWER THE CALL

1. In Romans 10:2 the Apostle Paul tells of Christians who have zeal for their faith, but a lack of knowledge of God and His Word. What specifically can you do on a consistent basis to avoid this same mistake? _____

_____

2. In Matthew 18:19, Jesus speaks of the power of agreement in prayer. Does this mean you can change through agreement how someone else acts or thinks?_____

_____

3. In the context of Ephesians 4:15 AMP, what actions should our lives reflect? Are there any areas you need to change?_____

_____

_____

4. According to Colossians 3:15, what is to decide with finality all of our questions? _____

_____

5. Why is it important to keep a clear conscience when praying for others? (See 1 Timothy 1:19.)_____

_____

_____

CHAPTER 13
LIFE BEYOND THE PRAYER CLOSET

You are the light of the world. A city set on a hill cannot be hid.

Nor do men light a lamp and put it under a bushel, but on a stand, and it gives light to all in the house. Let your light so shine before men, that they may see your good works and give glory to your Father who is in heaven.

Matthew 5:14-16 RSV

Many of my friends and I love the soft light of lit candles. Never do we hide flaming candles on the floor behind a sofa, but leave them out to create ambience. The soft candlelight creates an atmosphere of intimacy and relaxation.

As Christians our light is to grow brighter and brighter until it is like the full light of the noon day (Proverbs 4:18), and this emanates from within our hearts. Life in the prayer closet can insure a successful life beyond the prayer closet where men will see your good works and glorify the Father. God is interested in His children developing character and healthy relationships, for then we can "...give attentive, continuous care to watching over one another, studying how we may stir up (stimulate and incite) to love and helpful deeds and noble activities" (Hebrews 10:24 AMP). These relationships are born out of a productive prayer life.

In Matthew 6:9-13, Jesus gives us a prayer outline, commonly known as the Lord's Prayer. He continues His teaching on prayer with these words:

For if you forgive men when they sin against you, your heavenly Father will also forgive you. But if you do not forgive men their sins, your Father will not forgive your sins.

Matthew 6:14-15 NIV

In this verse Jesus connects prayer and forgiveness, an essential ingredient in the development of healthy relationships. Part of our life beyond the prayer closet is to walk consistently in love and forgiveness. When coming up against a stronghold or false mindset, we can be challenged to forgive. Thankfully prayer enables us to pull down strongholds that prohibit unity in private households as well as in the household of God.

Major Strongholds

Paul tells us that "...the weapons of our warfare are not carnal, but mighty through God to the pulling down of strong holds" (2 Corinthians 10:4). Strongholds, places of security or survival, are established in the mind. Many of these were developed during childhood as defenses against imaginary or actual dangerous emotional or physical situations. Even though our perceptions of events that took place may have been perverted and distorted, the strongholds are real. If carried over into adulthood, they sabotage what otherwise could be good, healthy relationships.

The tragedy is that past hurts and disappointments so often lead to unforgiveness, which is the greatest hindrance to answered prayer. Jesus spent most of His ministry preaching about the logistics of human relationships. He told His followers, "And whenever you stand praying, if you have anything against anyone, forgive him and let it drop (leave it, let it go), in order that your Father Who is in heaven may also forgive you your [own] failings and shortcomings and let them drop" (Mark 11:25 AMP).

You may have experienced times when you have talked with someone who could not hear or "understand" what you were saying. Later you may have discovered you had not heard the other person accurately either. You may have come up against a stronghold or mindset. These strongholds interfere with the voice of the Holy Spirit and divert us from the purpose and will of God in our prayer life, causing us to pray according to our own wishes. We may not be hearing what the Spirit is saying accurately; we may not understand His direction.

If your heart is truly after the things of God, then the Holy Spirit does not give up on you. He sends you the truth that enables you to pull down every stronghold, "Casting down imaginations, and every high thing that exalteth itself against the knowledge of God..." (2 Corinthians 10:5).

The enemy uses our strongholds of ignorance, prejudices, lusts, imaginations, carnal reasoning, and pride to keep us off-balance. (1 John 2:16.) *Holy Spirit, help us pray according to the will of God, not according to imaginations and unhealthy mindsets based on "doing our own thing," or instant gratification of our material desires.*

We do not attract others to the cross of Jesus when we try to manipulate them or insist on changing them according to our personal desires. Ask the Holy Spirit to help you recognize any strongholds of rigidity, denial, emotional isolation, or silence. Confess any sins with true repentance to the Father God. *Rigidity* renders a person inflexible, suppressing the ministry of our constant transformation. *Denial* opens the door for self-deception, repudiating the truth that sets us free. *Emotional isolation* causes us to be subject to hardness of heart, overruling our compassion for others. *Silence* stops the communication of our faith, preventing our true fellowship with God and man.

The Holy Spirit brings revelation, Jesus breaks down every wall of partition, and our Heavenly Father restores and brings salvation to our every destruction. He always wants you and me to be aware we represent Him right where we live, and wherever He sends us. These strongholds inhibit good communication skills, and hinder our testimony of a life of joy, peace, and victory.

ATTITUDES

In Matthew 6, Jesus speaks to His disciples about prayer:

And when you pray, do not be like the hypocrites, for they love to pray standing in the synagogues and on the street corners to be seen by men. I tell you the truth, they have received their reward in full. But when you pray, go into your room, close the door and pray to your Father, who is unseen. Then your Father, who sees what is done in secret, will reward you. And when you pray, do not keep on babbling like pagans, for they think they will be heard because of their many words. Do not be like them, for your Father knows what you need before you ask him.

Matthew 6:5-8 NIV

Here Jesus warns us of behaving as hypocrites who love to make a show of their religiosity. Jesus teaches us to go into the prayer closet—He promised that our Father who sees in secret will reward us openly. "Going into the prayer closet" is easily understood. Most conscientious believers are willing to follow these instructions about praying privately. How does God reward us openly? I believe that most of us who have prayed diligently for our families would say that our reward is noticeable behavioral "changes." We are free to love and no longer afraid of being vulnerable.

God desires to bring about changes in our homes, our communities, our nation, and the world as well as to develop within us the desire to live as fully mature followers of our Lord Jesus Christ. I walk with Jesus by taking up my cross and following Him. We are God's field under cultivation and He is constantly at work to help us produce fruit and more fruit, those godly characteristics that will influence others and draw them to Jesus Christ.

What does my behavior reflect to those with whom I come in contact? Do I wear my prayer life as a badge of self-righteousness where I am the only one who knows what godly behavior is? Have I become dogmatic, thinking that I'm always right and "they" are wrong? Has being right become more important than relationship?

Sometimes, it isn't the words you are speaking that are piercing, but the tone that is heard loud and clear. Oh my, I hate it when I hear "the tone" in my voice. It is a sign to me I haven't been in the house of the Lord beholding His beauty. Wrong attitudes and bad feelings toward others will override your desire to love as Jesus loves. Snobbery comes in many forms. My denomination is right and yours is wrong. When you feel superior to one group of people, there are others who leave you feeling inferior. Wrong attitudes and bad feelings toward others will cover up the light that could rejoice the heart of others. Isn't it wonderful to know that confessing our sin opens the door for His forgiveness and He remembers our sin no more?

God has said the spouse may be saved by the godly behavior of the believing spouse.[1] What does our behavior say about us? Do we wear our prayer life as a badge, proclaiming either overtly or subconsciously to all about our sacrificial life in the prayer closet; or do we demonstrate righteousness, peace, and joy in the Holy Ghost to our loved ones? We begin dealing truly by being honest with ourselves, by looking our attitudes squarely in the face, admitting when we are wrong, and asking forgiveness of those we have wronged.

It is our responsibility to be sensitive to the voice of God and responsive to His call to intercession both in the prayer closet and beyond. God wants to use us as channels of answered prayer. In our daily lives we exemplify the changes that took place through our diligent prayer time with the Father God.

BE A LIGHT IN YOUR COMMUNITY

I want to share one of the ways you can help in your community that is vital to the future of our nation.

Satan would like nothing better than to capture the minds of our children. Jesus loves the little children as the song says, "All the children of the world."[2] On an international level, we pray for children of other nations. There are children on the streets, children in foster homes, children who forage through garbage heaps and trash cans for food. There are children who are used as suicide bombers, and children who are sold for sexual purposes. There is evil and darkness all around. But I believe as the dark grows darker, the Light will shine brighter if we will pray and love others with the heart and compassion of the Father.

You only have to hear the news and read the papers to know there is a sense of fear hovering in the atmosphere. This began for us here in America a few years ago when students began killing students. The rate of suicides among young people increased and touched the lives of those we love. Bullying became more prevalent in schools, on school buses, and through the use of the Internet. Our children and teachers do not just hear about it on the news; most of them see and feel the effects of our country's moral decline in their current school environment. *Our school systems, children and teachers need our prayers.*

Our school system needs a spiritual revolution. Are you praying for your children and grandchildren's school systems; the school superintendents, administration, teachers and other personnel? Having talked with teachers, I realize how stressed and overloaded they can feel. The Bible gives us assurance that if we pray, our Father God will move mightily. 2 Chronicles 7:14 AMP says, "If My people, who are called by My name, shall humble themselves, pray, seek, crave, and require of necessity My face and turn from their wicked ways, then will I hear from heaven, forgive their sin, and heal their land." Our school systems need healing.

There is life beyond the prayer closet. Prayer isn't the only thing we can do but it is the most important. As we pray, God will hear from heaven and bring transformation to our school systems. If we really believe in the power of prayer, then we need to find time to pray.

When ungodly decisions rule a nation, the moral decline is on the march, especially in the lives of our children who are Satan's primary target, *but God!* His power is released as we pray.

"Blessed (happy, fortunate, to be envied) is the nation whose God is the Lord, the people He has chosen as His heritage" (Psalm 33:12 AMP). We must be committed to *praying* for our teachers. In addition to prayer, we also need to provide the *encouragement* and *cooperation* that teachers need to educate our children.

ENCOURAGE TEACHERS

Speak words of encouragement to teachers and treat them with respect. Encouragement refreshes and lifts emotions. It energizes people to do their best. 1 Thessalonians 5:11 says, "Therefore encourage one another and build each other up" (NIV). I salute qualified teachers who work countless hours. Their work isn't finished when the bell rings at the close of the school day, in fact, their work is far from over. I urge you to reach out to teachers with a word of encouragement. Teachers need to know that they are appreciated. They become rejuvenated when they know that their hard work is noticed. In addition, the Bible instructs us to love one another and give precedence and show honor to one another. (Romans 12:10.) I honor our schoolteachers who are working diligently to teach our children.

The teachers of our children and grandchildren cannot do the job of teaching and training them alone. They need us to partner with them to educate our children. As grandparents and parents, we have a responsibility to train up these precious children (our future generation) in the reverence and admonition of God—to teach them the ways of God. At one time the school systems reinforced godly principles without fear of reprisal; parents and teachers worked together for the good of the child. Even though the public schools do not allow God to be directly referred to in the classroom, we can still cooperate with our teachers to enable our students to be more successful. We must not expect the schools to take all the responsibility for a child's education. It grieves me when I hear parents blaming teachers for a child's lack of motivation and misbehavior. Is it really the teacher's fault when a child fails to apply himself/herself and puts forth no effort to get his/her schoolwork done?

TAKE RESPONSIBILITY AND MAKE A DIFFERENCE

Let us assume our responsibility and involve ourselves in the education of our children. Parents, let your child's teachers know you will work with them to build the character of your child. Years ago when my children were in school, they knew if they got in trouble at school, they would get in more trouble when they got home. We did not tolerate disrespect for authority figures, but held our children accountable for their own actions. (If we felt a teacher had been unfair, we discussed it with the teacher.) Parents, consider the wisdom of holding your children accountable to the authorities in their lives. As 1 Peter 5:5 explains: "Likewise you younger people, submit yourselves to your elders" (NKJV).

Dare to teach and train your children in the ways of God and introduce them to a God who loves them by demonstrating His love. Your children need to be taught right from wrong so they won't fall into the traps of the enemy. If you neglect to teach your children Truth someone else will take advantage and lead them in the way you would not have them go.

Ask the Holy Spirit to help you make your home a place where love reigns and wisdom is taught. Talk with your children and grandchildren, and listen to them. Let them know there is a way that leads to life, joy, and peace where they can receive the manifold blessings of God. He knew them before the foundation of the world, and He has chosen them for His very own, and He foreordained good things for their future.[3] Include Jeremiah 29:11-12 in your prayers for your children and grandchildren: "For I know the thoughts and plans that I have for you, says the Lord, thoughts and plans for welfare and peace and not for evil, to give you hope in your final outcome. Then you will call upon Me, and you will come and pray to Me, and I will hear and heed you" (AMP).

Most of our teachers are doing their best to promote a healthy learning environment. Nevertheless, there are self-centered people who hold jobs in our educational system who are not concerned with the proper development of our children. They are there to promote their own agendas or simply to draw a paycheck. Sometimes a child is abused, even sexually molested. These so-called teachers cannot stay hidden, and the best way that I know to deal with this problem is to pray for our school systems and the men and women who are in positions of authority. Pray that those who stand up for righteousness will be strong in the Lord and the power of His might. Come boldly before the throne of grace and find mercy and grace to help in time of need. Prayer will prepare you to speak out appropriately for the future good and welfare of the children. Let your voice be heard. There is life beyond the prayer closet.

The children of our nation are so important; please join me in praying for them, the teachers, and the school systems.

PRAYERS THAT AVAIL MUCH®
SCHOOL SYSTEMS AND CHILDREN

Father, we bring before You the _____ school system(s) and the men and women who are in positions of authority within the school system(s).

We ask You to give them skillful and godly wisdom, that Your knowledge might be pleasant to them. Then discretion will watch over them; understanding will keep them and deliver them from the way of evil and from evil men. We pray that men and women of integrity, blameless and complete in Your sight, remain in these positions, but that the wicked be cut off and the treacherous be rooted out in the name of Jesus.

Our children shrink from whatever might offend You, Father, and discredit the name of Christ. They show themselves to be blameless, guileless, innocent, and uncontaminated children of God, without blemish (faultless, unrebukable), in the midst of a crooked and wicked generation, holding out to it and offering to all the Word of Life. Thank You, Father, that You give them knowledge and skill in all learning and wisdom and bring them into favor with those around them.

Father, we pray and intercede that these young people, their parents, and the leaders in the school system(s) separate themselves from contact with contaminating and corrupting influences and cleanse themselves from everything that would contaminate and defile their spirits, souls, and bodies. We confess that they shun immorality and all sexual looseness—flee from impurity in thought, word, or deed—and they live and conduct themselves honorably and becomingly as in the open light of day. We confess and believe that they shun youthful lusts and flee from them.

Father, we ask You to commission the ministering spirits to go forth and police the area, dispelling the forces of darkness. Thank You for intercessors to stand on Your Word and for laborers of the harvest to preach Your Word in Jesus' name. Amen.

SCRIPTURE REFERENCES

Proverbs 2:10-12, 21-22 AMP; Philippians 2:15-16 AMP; Daniel 1:17 AMP; Daniel 1:9; 1 John 2:16-17 AMP; 2 Timothy 2:21 AMP; 2 Corinthians 7:1 AMP; 1 Corinthians 6:18 AMP; Romans 13:13 AMP; Ephesians 5:4; 2 Timothy 2:22; Matthew 18:18; 2 Timothy 2:26; Hebrew 1:14, Colossians 2:3 AMP

ANSWER THE CALL

1. What specifically do you think the light growing brighter in Proverbs 4:18 means to you? _____

_____

_____

2. The Apostle Paul says in 2 Corinthians 10:4 that we have the ability to pull down strongholds with the weapons of our warfare. What are those weapons? Have you ever used any of them on yourself or others? _____

_____

_____

3. In light of Matthew 6:5-8, are you pleased with how your behavior is perceived by those closest to you? _____

_____

_____

4. In Matthew 5:14 Jesus says believers are the light of the world. How can you be a light in your community? _____

_____

_____

CHAPTER 14
CHRIST AND HIS CHURCH

C ertain aspects of the true Church of Jesus Christ provide us with our confidence in His victory for a glorious world in the Kingdom of God, in the spiritual realm, and in eternity to come. Initially we need to know about the foundation of the Church, our responsibility in it, and we need to examine various Scriptures which relate to it as the Lord leads us.

"WHO AM I?"

When Jesus came into the coasts of Caesarea Philippi, he asked his disciples, saying, Whom do men say that I the Son of man am?

And they said, Some say that thou art John the Baptist: some, Elias; and others, Jeremias, or one of the prophets.

He saith unto them, But whom say ye that I am?

226 • A Global Call to Prayer

And Simon Peter answered and said, Thou art the
Christ, the Son of the living God.

And Jesus answered and said unto him, Blessed
art thou, Simon Barjona: for flesh and blood hath
not revealed it unto thee, but my Father which is
in heaven. And I say also unto thee, That thou art
Peter [a fragment of a rock], and upon this rock [an
immovable stone, Christ Jesus Himself] I will build my
church; and the gates of hell shall not prevail against it.

Matthew 16:13-18 (parentheses mine)

Jesus not only promises that He will build the Church, but He
also promises that the gates of hell shall not prevail against it. This
signifies that we as Christians are already winners in the face of all
opposition to the Gospel of Christ.

Jesus has already given us authority and power over all the
power of the devil and we are the enforcers of His triumphant
victory. When He gave His Church the keys to the Kingdom, He,
in fact, gave the ability, the power and the authority to overcome
all the strategies of the enemy. Jesus gave us the keys to the
Kingdom of Heaven—and whatsoever we bind on earth will be
bound in heaven; and whatsoever we loose on earth shall be loosed
in heaven. (Matthew 18:18.)

JESUS, THE SON OF GOD

First let's ask, "Who do we say that Jesus is?" Isn't it wonderful through the revelation knowledge given to Peter, and also given to us, we can know Jesus is the Son of the Living God? This Jesus is the Captain of our salvation and He leads us in His triumphant victory over the adversary. The very foundation of our prayer life is based on the question: Who do we say that Jesus is?

JESUS, THE FOUNDER OF
THE CHURCH

The second question to ask is, "Who is building the Church?" Jesus! He says that He will build His Church. In Matthew 16:16-18 Peter says to Jesus: "Thou art the Christ, the Son of the living God." Jesus responds: "Upon this rock I will build my church." This was a disclosure of Himself, the Rock of Ages.

On the day of Pentecost, Peter spoke forth a proclamation of this revelation, bringing deliverance and salvation to three thousand souls.[1] It was Simon Peter who later called Jesus a "living stone" (1 Peter 2:4), the "chief cornerstone" (v. 6), a "stone of stumbling" and a "rock of offence" (v. 8). Then it was Peter who defined believers as "lively stones" (v. 5).

The Church is built upon the foundation of the apostles and prophets, Jesus Christ Himself being the chief cornerstone.

(Ephesians 2:19-22.) We are the Church and the Church of Jesus Christ is made up of people whom Peter calls "lively stones."

LIVELY STONES

The term "lively stones" implies that we are in the process of building something as well as being built into a structure, a dwelling place of God. Jesus has assumed His responsibility in building the Church. He firmly joins and firmly knits us together as each "stone" works properly in all its functions, growing up to full maturity, and building up one another in love. (Ephesians 4:16.)

Now it is time for us to assume our responsibility as members of the household of faith. Through intercession we repair breaches, restore streets to dwell in, and build up a highway that leads from Satan's domain to life and peace, reconciliation and salvation—the Kingdom of God. (Isaiah 58:12; Ezekiel 22:30.) It was Isaiah who cried, "Go through, go through the gates; prepare ye the way of the people, cast up, cast up the highway; gather out the stones; lift up a standard for the people" (Isaiah 62:10). Not only are we building highways of deliverance, but also we are making up a "wall" by filling up any "gap" which may appear in the wall around those for whom we are praying.

God Himself is our shield; He is our fortress, and He is our fortification; but we are the lively stones that make up the wall and overthrow the plots of the evil one. Jesus is building His house.

REBUILDING THE WALL

We turn to the Old Testament for a look at the rebuilding of Jerusalem where worship was restored after the return of the Jews from Babylon. In the Book of Nehemiah, it was the people who built the wall and God who fought their battle against their enemies. Even though there was great opposition to the building of the wall round about Jerusalem, it was completed.

It is interesting that when the Israelites began to build the wall, the enemy became very upset; Sanballat was "...wroth, and took great indignation, and mocked the Jews" (Nehemiah 4:1) and Tobiah, the Ammonite, declared even a fox could break down their wall by simply walking on top of it (v. 3).

When you and I begin a work for the Kingdom of God, the enemy makes it his business to throw obstacles into our paths. However, we are lively stones, strong in the Lord and the power of His might. (Ephesians 6:10.) We are not ignorant concerning the devices of the evil one. (2 Corinthians 2:11.) Nehemiah tells us:

Those who built the wall and those who bore burdens loaded themselves so that every one worked with one hand and held a weapon with the other hand, and every builder had his sword girded by his side, and so worked. And he who sounded the trumpet was at my side.

Nehemiah 4:17-18

In the New Testament we discover that God through Christ Jesus has fought our battle. Jesus is building His Church; we are co-laborers together with Him; and the Holy Spirit has been sent to aid and bear us up in our inability to produce results. We do not always know which prayer to offer or how to offer it as worthily as we ought. In our inabilities or weaknesses God's strength is made perfect. That which is impossible with man is possible with God. We believers have no reason to be afraid of the enemy for God is on our side. We stand in readiness for the attacks of the enemy, loaded with the armor of God and our sword, the Word of God. (Ephesians 6.)

The Holy Spirit knows where the enemy is attacking and gives the trumpet sound—our call to pray. Our enemies cannot be seen with the natural eye. You and I are not battling against flesh and blood; we are not praying against people. Remember, our fight is "the good fight of the faith" (1 Timothy 6:12) which takes place in the realm of the Spirit. We take our stand against principalities, against powers, against the rulers of the darkness of this world, and wicked spirits in heavenly places. (Ephesians 6:12.) Having done all to stand, we stand firm in our faith that Jesus Christ is Lord!

RECONCILERS TO TRUTH

As intercessors we are a vital part of life transformations—reconcilers to truth. Humbly we receive the word planted in our hearts that sets us free from all our own destructions. We are empowered to lay aside every weight that would hinder us. It is imperative that we live a lifestyle of prayer "speaking truly, dealing truly, living truly" (Ephesians 4:15 AMP).

Peter defines the approach to this lifestyle in 1 Peter 2:1, "So get rid of your feelings of hatred. Don't just pretend to be good! Be done with dishonesty and jealousy and talking about others behind their backs" (TLB).

It is our responsibility to guard our hearts and recognize people are not our problem. One of the most successful strategies of the devil is sowing discord among the believers through the power of thoughtless words often spoken by wounded believers. His objective is to divide and conquer—to set husband against wife, brother against brother, and sister against sister. Therefore, we have to lay aside all malice, all guile, all hypocrisies, envies and all evil speaking.[2] We are to hold the thoughts, feelings and purposes of God's heart. God has said that His grace is sufficient for us (2 Corinthians 12:9), and it is His grace that enables us to obey the Scriptures.

SPEAKING, DEALING, AND LIVING TRULY

Allowing we may have rationalized our intentions and played mind games with ourselves, it takes the work of the Holy Spirit within us to expose malice and ill will toward others. A necessary ingredient in effectual prayer strategy (a truth which I believe cannot be repeated too often) is that we always "speak truly, deal truly, and live truly" (Ephesians 4:15 AMP).

This does not mean pointing the finger at the other fellow (trying to remove the splinter that is in his eye), but taking moral inventory of ourselves (removing the plank that is in our own eye).[3] We do not wait until we are perfect to pray but we purpose to have right attitudes and pure hearts. Let us destroy all strongholds—all man-made defenses developed when we have unhealed hurts and unresolved issues.

It is particularly easy for us to involve ourselves in hypocrisies and spiritual pride when we are spiritually immature and emotionally crippled. Hidden hurts and unacknowledged anger are opposing perspectives that will dominate and control us, causing us to give in to our own systematic rigidity and deception. Keep alert and constantly guard against dogmatic, judgmental, and critical attitudes lest we give place to the devil[4] and our prayers be hindered. Entering into the prayer of praise and thanksgiving, and offering our bodies as living sacrifices will give us spiritual weapons to displace thoughts that are contrary to the Word of God about ourselves and others.

CHRISTIAN MATURITY

Mature Christians are to bear the weaknesses of others, keeping their hearts pure, desiring "the sincere milk of the Word that ye may grow thereby" (1 Peter 2:2). It is by the Word of God we mature, being constantly renewed in the spirit of our mind (Romans 12:2)—having a fresh mental and spiritual attitude which displaces strongholds and man-made defenses that interfere with true intercession.

We are precious in God's Kingdom, and it is our responsibility to walk in that which He has provided for us. He has provided us with both relationship and position. Our relationship with God and man is "servant," but also our position is "priest" in a holy priesthood:

If so be ye have tasted that the Lord is gracious. To whom coming, as unto a living stone, disallowed indeed of men, but chosen of God, and precious, Ye also, as lively stones, are built up a spiritual house, an holy priesthood, to offer up spiritual sacrifices, acceptable to God by Jesus Christ.

1 Peter 2:3-5

Therefore, one of the first principles of intercessory prayer is our recognition we are a holy priesthood, and our first attention is the offering of praise and worship to our God. We are members of a holy priesthood by His grace.

Learn to appropriate the garment of praise to usher you into the place of victorious intercession. Many opposing forces are sent to overcome you and destroy your effectiveness in the Kingdom of

God. Praise will stop and still the avenger who has come to deter you and cause you to faint, lose heart, or give up. Preparing for intercession through praise enables you to speak the Word which goes forth like a guided missile and hits its target.

THE GARMENT OF PRAISE

There was a time when I had grown weary in well-doing. It seemed the very life of God was drained from me. Early one Sunday I was trying to prepare myself for the morning service when the phone rang. It was my mom, saying, "Germaine, I received today's church bulletin in the mail yesterday. Now do what it says to do." I promised her I would pray the prayer of commitment, "To Rejoice in the Lord."[5]

Believe me, I did not feel like praying; I did not feel like ministering to anyone; and I certainly did not feel like praising. Very feebly I began to rejoice in the Lord. As I continued, I became stronger and stronger. As I began swinging my arms, shouting, and dancing all over my kitchen, the spirit of heaviness left and I was clothed in the garment of praise.

You have to have a made-up mind to praise and worship God. The enemy would like to silence you—to keep you quiet: "From the lips of children and infants you have ordained praise because of your enemies, to silence the foe and the avenger" (Psalm 8:2 NIV).

The word "praise" also means "strength." The Psalmist David was not quiet in his praise to his God. Joyous people in the Scriptures were not a silent people—they made a joyful noise unto the Rock of their salvation. (Psalm 95:1.) "O clap your hands, all ye people; shout unto God with the voice of triumph" (Psalm 47:1). Again and again David admonishes the people of his day, "Sing praises to God, sing praises unto our King, sing praises" (Psalm 47:6). In Psalm 34:1 David writes, "I will bless the LORD at all times: his praise shall continually be in my mouth."

If you will praise the Lord, the Holy Spirit will give you new songs that you have never heard before. The Holy Spirit, your Teacher, will bring New Testament Scriptures into focus as you speak to yourself "...in psalms and hymns and spiritual songs, singing and making melody in your heart to the Lord" (Ephesians 5:19).

Then, out of the abundance of the heart, the mouth speaks. (Luke 6:45.) If it's in your heart, it will come out your mouth. Release the glad heart and joyous spirit God has given you. Worshipping in spirit and in truth applies pressure to the rivers of living water that flow out of your innermost being like a mighty life stream.

Don't wait until you feel like it before you begin praising the Lord. Do it because the Bible says to and you will find that you have joined a heavenly host who are praising God in the highest. Holy, Holy, is the Lord!

Begin your day by proclaiming praises unto your Father:

PRAYERS OF PRAISE

Father, this is the day that You have made. I will rejoice and be glad in it! That spirit of rejoicing, joy and laughter is my heritage. I will praise You with joyful lips. I am ever filled and stimulated by the Holy Spirit. Where Your Spirit is, Lord, there is liberty—emancipation from bondage and freedom. I walk in that liberty.

I speak out in psalms and hymns and make melody with all my heart to You. My happy heart is a good medicine and my cheerful mind works healing. Your joy is my strength. Therefore, I can count it all joy, all strength, when I encounter tests or trials of any sort because I am strong in You, Lord, and in the power of Your might.

I have the victory in the Name of Jesus. Satan is under Jesus' feet. I will not be moved by adverse circumstances.

Most of the time, entering into a time of intercessory prayer follows praise and worship to God. (Not always, we can't be dogmatic about these things.) It is the Holy Spirit who leads us and helps us pray effectively. He knows where intercession is needed and He strengthens us when we take our stand against the opposing forces of darkness.

Ask the Holy Spirit to teach you how to place yourself in a position to hear and recognize His voice. I believe He is constantly attempting to lead the followers of Jesus. The reason we have to spend time in praise and worship is so we can quiet our minds and position ourselves to hear what the Holy Spirit is saying.

ANSWER THE CALL

1. Jesus says in Matthew 16:18, "I will build my church; and the gates of hell shall not prevail against it." How does this statement affect your prayer life? _____

_____

2. The Apostle Peter defines believers as "lively stones" (1 Peter 2:5). What does it mean to you to be a "lively stone?" (See Ephesians 4:16.)_____

_____

3. What does it mean to "fight the good fight of faith" (1 Timothy 6:12, Ephesians 6:12)? _____

_____

4. What can you do the fulfill Paul's admonition to "renew your mind" in Romans 12:1-2? _____

_____

5. In Ephesians 5:19 we are encouraged to sing and praise the Lord. Is this something you do on a regular basis? How you can work praise into your day? _____

_____

CHAPTER 15
MEMBERS OF A
ROYAL PRIESTHOOD

But you are a chosen race, a royal priesthood, a dedicated nation, [God's] own purchased, special people, that you may set forth the wonderful deeds and display the virtues and perfections of Him Who called you out of darkness into His marvelous light.

Once you were not a people [at all], but now you are God's people; once you were unpitied, but now you are pitied *and* have received mercy.

1 Peter 2:9-10 AMP

Doesn't this shout volumes about God's love for you? This priesthood is not out of the pages of the Old Testament but flows out of our relationship with Jesus. In the fifth verse of chapter two, Peter tells us that we are a "holy priesthood."

Then in verse 9 he calls believers a "royal priesthood." Wow! What is the meaning of this? If I believe what Peter is saying here what does it require of me? How can I possibly fulfill such a lofty position as this? I turn to the Old Testament for understanding.

As followers of Christ we have a standing invitation to come into the throne room. In the pages of the Old Testament we see that once a year the high priest, only, could go into the holy place of the temple where he met with God.[1] It was said of Aaron by the Lord in Exodus 28:29 "...Aaron shall bear the names of the children of Israel in the breastplate of judgment upon his heart, when he goeth in unto the holy place, for a memorial before the LORD continually."

The high priest acted as a mediator—an intercessor—on behalf of all the people, appearing before God for them. An intercessor is one who prays for others. The priests were the designated intercessors of the Old Testament. Since you and I belong to the priesthood, we are all empowered to pray and intercede for others.

Priests were constantly reminded of their allotted intercession. The names of the tribes of Israel were engraved on precious stones attached to the ephod and the breastplate which were parts of the priestly robe. The high priest bore the burden of the people upon his shoulders and heart to identify with their need for intercession. His prayers on behalf of the people were his perpetual assignment.[2]

What has God placed upon your heart? It is He who assigns, He places "prayer burdens" upon the heart—some for a short period of time, others to be more persistent.

Intercession on behalf of your government, your family, your church, or the nations of the world for instance, is an extended prayer assignment. Sometimes you will find yourself praying regularly for a specific nation or ministry. One lady prays every day for the Jewish people and is acutely interested in reading or viewing anything she finds concerning them. She has already visited the Holy Land, and desires to return to Israel. The names of people or their faces may come before you as a prompting from the Holy Spirit calling you to prayer. At times you may intercede momentarily for someone known or unknown.

THE POWER OF GOD'S LOVE

Paul doesn't present a thesis on intercessory prayer but when I read the books he wrote I know that he prayed for others. His passion for the Jewish people presents me with a challenge, and I would like to skip over the ninth chapter of Romans, but I can't. You can't miss his meaning:

> At the same time, you need to know that I carry
> with me at all times a huge sorrow. It's an enormous
> pain deep within me, and I'm never free of it. I'm

not exaggerating—Christ and the Holy Spirit are my witnesses. It's the Israelites... If there were any way I could be cursed by the Messiah so they could be blessed by him, I'd do it in a minute. They're my family. I grew up with them. They had everything going for them—family, glory, covenants, revelation, worship, promises, to say nothing of being the race that produced the Messiah, the Christ, who is God over everything, always. Oh, yes!

Romans 9:1-5, MSG

When I read this passage of Scripture I would like to ignore Paul's meaning. I stop and ask myself if I love anyone as much as Paul loved and longed for his people to know Christ, to know their God. Would I be willing to be accursed, go to hell, for anyone? Am I serious about the redemption and salvation of others? How long will it take for me to let go of self-importance and realize apart from the love of God, I would be absorbed with getting my needs met rather than esteeming others as better than myself? Praise God I am not apart from the love of God.

If God loved me enough to come to my house when I had deliberately made a decision that I didn't want anything to do with Him, wouldn't He reach out to the infidel, the abortionist, the homosexual, the bum on the street, the alcoholic, and drug addict? Don't forget Jesus died for the salvation and redemption of all mankind.

When I was growing up I constantly felt defeated because I couldn't keep all the rules of my church. I thought when I failed that I had failed God and self-hatred was born; I knew I was headed for eternal damnation. Every time I got "saved" I hoped that it would last. Some Christians demand that others keep their rules, fit into the culture of the church, even while they themselves, not to mention wounded Christians, can't live up to the church's expectations.

Keeping rules didn't work, but when I fell in love with Jesus, I was changed on the inside and my behavior began to change day by day. Transformation was by the Spirit of God, and when I failed, I learned I had not forfeited my relationship with God. I reasoned if He loves me unconditionally, He loves all mankind unconditionally. Yes, He hates evil and I hate the evil that keeps mankind in bondage, constantly trying to meet his own needs. All mankind needs a Savior, and God included the prayers of His children in His plan for humanity.

How can I love as Jesus loved? He gave His all; am I willing to give my all? True mediation cannot be wrapped up in a pretty package with a bow on it. There is a price to be paid to walk in the steps of a holy and royal priest. Most intercession is hidden from others in the Body of Christ, but it is not hidden from the Father. There may be no accolades in this world for those who are hidden away in prayer, giving their lives for the salvation of others, but we can rejoice in that we have done the will of God in the earth. When there is an answer to prayer, all the glory goes to God, and we receive the victory. (1 John 5:4.) It's all by His grace heaped upon grace.

WALK AS A CHILD OF LIGHT

I challenge you to go forth as reformers walking in the light and as children of light, imitate your Father who is in heaven. (Ephesians 5:1.) "Let your light so shine before men that they may see your moral excellence and your praiseworthy, noble, and good deeds and recognize and honor and praise and glorify your Father Who is in heaven" (Matthew 5:16 AMP).

Remember, the seeds of prayer you have sown on behalf of others will profit you—will change your false beliefs—will destroy your past defenses and enable you to fulfill your ministry of reconciliation. Go beyond your own little world and reach out to the rest of the globe in your prayers. Expect God to lead your prayer life to touch the world—in the salvation of nations, politics, schools, governments, and more! Since before the foundation of the world God has been preparing for this moment in time. Your birth was not an accident. You were born for such a time as this!

NOTES

CHAPTER 1

[1]John 15:12

[2]Matt. 6:6

[3]"What the World Needs Now is Love" by Burt Bacharach and Hal David (Imperial Records, 1965).

[4]"We've a Story to Tell to the Nations" Text: H. Ernest Nichol, 1862-1928 (CWH attrib to Colin Sterne) Music: H. Ernest Nichol, 1862-1928.

[5]Romans 8:37

[6]Ephesians 3:21

CHAPTER 2

[1]Germaine Copeland and Lane Holland, *Prayers That Avail Much for Leaders*, (Tulsa, Oklahoma: Harrison House 2008), 131.

[2]Matthew 6:10

CHAPTER 3

[1]Philippians 4:19

[2]Ephesians 6:18

[3]Ezekiel 22:30

[4]2 Corinthians 4:18

CHAPTER 4

[1]"Just As I Am", words by Charlotte Elliott, 1835. Music by William Bradbury, 1849.

[2]Matthew 6:9

[3]Ephesians 2:10

[4]Psalm 23:4

[5]Psalm 144:15

[6]"I'll Be Somewhere Listening for My Name" by Bill Anderson, Amazing Grace (2008, Goldenlane Records).

[7]Ephesians 5:22-33

CHAPTER 5

[1]Psalm 16:11

[2]2 Corinthians 3:17

[3]1 Thessalonians 5:17

[4]Matthew 5:37

[5]Luke 18:1

CHAPTER 7

[1]Derek Prince, *Secrets of a Prayer Warrior* (Grand Rapids: Chosen Books, A Division of Baker Publishing Group, 2009), 79.

[2]Kenneth Nathaniel Taylor, *The Living Bible Paraphrased* (Carol Stream: Tyndal House Publishers, 1971.)

[3]Luke 22:32

[4]Colossians 1:3-4

[5]commend. 2010. In *Merriam-Webster Online Dictionary.* Retrieved March 13, 2010, from http://www.merriam-webster.com/dictionary/commend

[6]Saint Therese of Lisieux, translated by John Beevers, *The Autobiography of Saint Therese of Lisieux, The Story of a Soul,* (New York: Doubleday, a division of Random House, Inc., 1957), X.

CHAPTER 8

[1]1 Timothy 1:18

[2]Rick Renner, *Dressed to Kill* (Tulsa, Oklahoma: Teach All Nations, 1991, 2007), 18.

[3]Derek Prince, *Secrets of a Prayer Warrior* (Grand Rapids: Chosen Books, A Division of Baker Publishing Group, 2009), 73.

[4]C. S. Lewis, *The Screwtape Letters, a C. S. Lewis Treasury* (Uhrichsville, Ohio: Barbour Publishing, 1990), 213.

[5]W. E. Vine, *Vine's Complete Expository Dictionary of Old and New Testament Words* (Nashville: Thomas Nelson Publishers, 1996), 688.

[6]sway. (2010). In Merriam-Webster Online Dictionary. Retrieved March 14, 2010, from http://www.merriam-webster.com/dictionary/sway

[7]ibid

[8]vibrate. (2009). *Webster's New World College Dictionary* (Cleveland, Ohio: Wiley Publishing, Inc., used by arrangement with John Wiley & Sons, Inc.)Retrieved

March 14, 2010 from http://www.yourdictionary.com/
vibrate

⁹ibid

CHAPTER 9

¹Effectual prayer. 1897. *Easton's Bible Dictionary.* Retrieved
March 15, 2010, from http://www.biblegateway.
com/resources/dictionaries/dict_meaning
php?source=1&wid=T0001132

²Lamentations 3:22-23

³Liberty Savard, *Shattering Your Strongholds* (Alachua,
FL: Bridge-Logos Foundation, 1993).

⁴Isaiah 55:11

⁵Thayer and Smith. "Greek Lexicon entry for Homologia".
The New Testament Greek Lexicon. Retrieved May 18, 2010,
from <http://www.studylight.org/lex/grk/view
cgi?number=3671>

⁶W. E. Vine, *Vine's Complete Expository Dictionary of Old and
New Testament Words* (Nashville: Thomas Nelson
Publishers, 1996), 324.

CHAPTER 10

¹Galatians 4:19

²Saint Therese of Lisieux, translated by John Beevers, *The
Autobiography of Saint Therese of Lisieux, The Story of a Soul,*
(New York: Doubleday, a division of Random House, Inc.,
1957), X.

³1 Corinthians 2:16

⁴2 Corinthians 1:20

⁵Thayer and Smith. "Greek Lexicon entry for Odino". The New Testament Greek Lexicon. Retrieved May 18, 2010, from <http://www.studylight.org/lex/grk/view.cgi?number=5605>.

⁶Philippians 4:7

⁷Kerby Anderson, *Decline of a Nation* (Plano, Texas: Probe Ministries, 1991). Retrieved May 18, 2010, from http://www.leaderu.com/orgs/probe/docs/decline.html.

⁸2 Chronicles 7:14 AMP

⁹Philip Yancey, *Prayer, Does It Make Any Difference* (Grand Rapids, Michigan: Zondervan, 2006), 130.

CHAPTER 11

¹Charles W. Conn, *Like a Mighty Army* (Cleveland, TN: Pathway Press, 1994).

²ibid, 40.

⁵glossolalia. (2010). *In Merriam-Webster Online Dictionary.* Retrieved March 20, 2010, from http://www.merriam-webster.com/dictionary/glossolalia

⁵Rick Renner, *Dressed to Kill* (Tulsa, Oklahoma: Teach All Nations, 1991, 2007), 18.

⁵Howard Carter, *Questions and Answers on Spiritual Gifts* (Tulsa, Oklahoma: Harrison House, 1991), 145.

⁶ibid

⁷Author Unknown, "Somewhere in the Shadows"

(Copyright unknown).

[8]George Bennard, "The Old Rugged Cross." 1913.

CHAPTER 12

[1]Rick Renner, *Dressed to Kill* (Tulsa, Oklahoma: Teach All Nations, 1991, 2007), 67.

[2]C. S. Lewis, *The Screwtape Letters, a C. S. Lewis Treasury* (Uhrichsville, Ohio: Barbour Publishing, 1990).

[3]John 10:4

[4]Matt 6:8-10

[5]John 16:13

CHAPTER 13

[1]1 Corinthians 7:14-16

[2]Author unknown, "Jesus Loves the Little Children." n.d.

[3]Ephesians 1:4-5

CHAPTER 14

[1]Acts 2:14-41

[2]1 Peter 2:1

[3]Matthew 7:4

[4]Ephesians 4:27

[5]Germaine Copeland, *Prayers That Avail Much, Volume 1* (Tulsa, Oklahoma: Harrison House, 1999), 47.

CHAPTER 15

[1]Exodus 30:10

[2]Exodus 28

ADDITIONAL RESOURCES:

Dietrich Bonhoeffer, *The Cost of Discipleship* (New York, Macmillan, 1959)

Brother Lawrence, *The Practice of the Presence of God* (Xulon Press, 2007)

Richard Foster, *Celebration of Discipline* (San Francisco: HarperSanFrancisco, 1988)

Richard J. Foster, editor, *The Renovare Spiritual Formation Bible* (Harper One, 2006)

Arthur Wallis, *God's Chosen Fast* (Fort Washington, Pa: Christian Literature Crusade, 1971)

APPENDIX

FASTING

By Lane Holland, MSN, M.Div.

When it comes to the topic of fasting it seems the Church has divergent opinions about the matter. Most agree it is biblically based but intense discussions begin when we try to find meaning for this spiritual discipline in today's communities of faith. The conversations range from the need for basic information on the subject to just how disciplined one should be when it comes to fasting. Should we fast one day a week, two days, once a month, or only when the pastor calls a corporate fast?

In its purest form, fasting serves to move the believer closer to God. The words of Jesus in the Gospel declare, "Man shall not live by bread alone, but by every word that proceedeth out of the mouth of God" (Matthew 4:4). In his book, *Growing in the Life of Faith: Education and Christian Practices*, Craig Dykstra states, "The practices and disciplines are means of grace, not tasks to accomplish or instructions to follow in order to grow in the life of faith."[1] Fasting can help when we need to have keen discernment and know God's will for our lives. Fasting is also instrumental in helping us learn to listen to what He calls us to be and do in the world.

The following is a brief overview of the definition, history, discipline, and development of a fasting lifestyle. I will conclude with some practical guidelines for the beginner and encouragement for those who have consistently included fasting in their spiritual walk. There are several resources listed at the end if you would like to do a more in depth study of the practice.

DEFINITION

Fasting is more than going without food. It serves to quiet all of our "external voices" so we can hear our "internal voice" or the Spirit of God more clearly. The most basic definition for fasting is to abstain from all food. Another definition is an abstinence from food, or a limiting of one's food, especially when voluntary and as a religious observance.[2]

For most Christian communities the idea of fasting is usually connected with times of prayer, meditation, and bible study. In some faith communities around the world, fasting is at times done as a "shut-in," which is spending the time of the fast in a facility (church, monastery, or retreat center) away from all distractions for the duration of the fast. The shut-in should, if possible, be accompanied with set times of prayer and study of the Scriptures. In his book, *Celebration of Discipline*, Richard Foster believes fasting is "the only way we will be saved from loving the blessing more than the Blesser."[3]

Fasting is an expression of and an exercise in humility. In the book of Leviticus, fasting is described as a time of "afflicting the soul" which signifies the individual has humbled themselves in the presence of God. (See Leviticus 23:27, 29, 32.) Fasting is the way a believer gives a wholehearted "yes" to God for whatever His will is in a given situation. One of the most definitive examples of this is found in 2 Samuel 12:15-20 when David's son by Bathsheba was sick. David's response following the death of his son showed his acceptance of God's purpose and destiny for him:

> And the LORD struck the child that Uriah's wife bore to David, and it became ill. David therefore pleaded with God for the child, and David fasted and went in and lay all night on the ground. So the elders of his house arose and went to him, to raise him up from the ground. But he would not, nor did he eat food with them. Then on the seventh day it came to pass that the child died. And the servants of David were afraid to tell him that the child was dead. For they said, "Indeed, while the child was alive, we spoke to him, and he would not heed our voice. How can we tell him that the child is dead? He may do some harm!"
>
> When David saw that his servants were whispering, David perceived that the child was dead. Therefore David said to his servants, "Is the child dead?"
>
> And they said, "He is dead."
>
> So David arose from the ground, washed and anointed himself, and changed his clothes; and he went into the house of the LORD and worshiped. Then he went to his own house; and when he requested, they set food before him, and he ate (NKJV).

Fasting is only one of the disciplines that help us to be transformed into the image and likeness of Jesus Christ. It is a way of crying out like the Psalmist, "Create in me a clean heart, O God; and renew a right spirit within me" (Psalm 51:10). It is the path to being "renewed day by day" (2 Corinthians 4:16).

HISTORY FROM THE OLD TESTAMENT

First, let fasting be done unto the Lord with our eye singly fixed on Him. Let our intention herein be this, and this alone, to glorify our Father which is in heaven.[4]

This quote from John Wesley (found in the collection *Sermons On Several Occasions*) helps to establish the fact that fasting has almost always been a part of the New Testament Church. It may have had different forms and significance during different periods of church history but was regarded as beneficial to spiritual growth and development.

If we study the Old Testament we find enough references to fasting to establish it as a legitimate part of spiritual life. Some familiar names connected with fasting include Moses, Elijah, David, Esther, Nehemiah, and Daniel.

And I set my face unto the Lord God, to seek by prayer and supplications, with fasting, and sackcloth, and ashes.

Daniel 9:3

The entire nation of Israel was commanded to fast on the Day of Atonement. When impending disasters or crises faced Israel, their leaders called for fasting. One such example is found in 2 Chronicles 20:1-4. King Jehoshaphat is facing war with the surrounding nations and calls for a fast:

After this, the armies of the Moabites, Ammonites, and some of the Meunites declared war on Jehoshaphat. Messengers came and told Jehoshaphat, "A vast army from Edom is marching against you from beyond the Dead Sea. They are already at Hazazon-tamar." (This was another name for En-gedi.) Jehoshaphat was terrified by this news and begged the LORD for guidance. He also ordered everyone in Judah *to begin fasting*. So people from all the towns of Judah came to Jerusalem to seek the LORD's help. (Emphasis mine, NLT)

In the book of Jonah 3:6-10 the people of Nineveh and their king proclaim a fast petitioning God for mercy when Jonah delivers to them the pronouncement of impending destruction that is only forty days away. When God sees the people fast and repent, He has mercy on them and does not destroy them.

In unusual circumstances it is possible for fasting to put us in a position to hear clearly the voice of God. As we receive His Word to us, He is able to release forgiveness, restoration, wisdom, faith, and strength.

Again in another instance, the depth of God's love for His people is demonstrated through the mercy extended to one of the kings of Judah when he humbled himself before God:

And the LORD spake to Manasseh, and to his people: but they would not hearken. Wherefore the LORD brought upon them the captains of the host of the king of Assyria, which took Manasseh among the thorns, and bound him with fetters, and carried him to

Babylon. And when he was in affliction, he besought the LORD his God, and humbled himself greatly before the God of his fathers, And prayed unto him: and he was intreated of him, and heard his supplication, and brought him again to Jerusalem into his kingdom. Then Manasseh knew that the LORD he was God.

2 Chronicles 33:10-13

One final example from the Old Testament is found in the book of Ezra 8:21-23 when the prophet Ezra began the journey to Jerusalem:

And there by the Ahava Canal, I gave orders for all of us *to fast and humble ourselves* before our God. We prayed that he would give us a safe journey and protect us, our children, and our goods as we traveled. For I was ashamed to ask the king for soldiers and horsemen to accompany us and protect us from enemies along the way. After all, we had told the king, "Our God's hand of protection is on all who worship him, but his fierce anger rages against those who abandon him." *So we fasted and earnestly prayed* that our God would take care of us, and he heard our prayer. (Emphasis mine, NLT)

In each of these instances fasting is connected with prayer and a posture of humility before God. Whether that posture was actually physical with sackcloth and ashes as seen in Jonah's story or a spiritual one, it is evident there is a bending of the heart, mind, and soul toward a benevolent God.

HISTORY FROM THE NEW TESTAMENT

In the New Testament we can also find references to fasting. Anna, the prophetess, served the Lord day and night in the temple with fastings and prayer. (Luke 2:36-37.) We see Jesus fasting as recorded in Matthew 4:1-11 and Luke 4:1-13. Christ spent a period of forty days and nights fasting. The Scriptures teach He was led into the wilderness to be tempted by Satan and His ability to endure was through the affliction of His soul. In Matthew 6:16-18 Jesus teaches on fasting during what we call the Sermon on the Mount. In His teaching Jesus uses the word "when" as opposed to "if" in regards to fasting, suggesting His disciples would utilize this particular spiritual discipline.

Jesus also gives us a key for times when prayer doesn't seem to change situations. In the case of the child His disciples could not cure, Jesus teaches them additional insight would come with both prayer and fasting. (Matthew 17:15-21.)

In the book of Acts, the early Church finds help for major decisions through combining prayer with fasting. Before major missionary endeavors and in the establishment of the churches, wisdom is sought through times of prayer and fasting. We are not told how long they fasted and prayed, just that the direction of the church is birthed with both fasting and prayer: "As they ministered to the Lord, and fasted, the Holy Ghost said, Separate me Barnabas and Saul for the work whereunto I have called them. And when they had fasted and prayed, and laid their hands on them, they sent them away" (Acts 13:2-3).

In Acts 14:23 another reference is made to fasting and prayer: "And when they had ordained them elders in every church, and had prayed with fasting, they commended them to the Lord, on whom they believed."

The Apostle Paul gave instructions to married couples regarding their times of fasting in his first letter to the Corinthian believers: "Defraud ye not one the other, except it be with consent for a time, that ye may give yourselves to fasting and prayer; and come together again, that Satan tempt you not for your incontinency" (1 Corinthians 7:5).

Church history shows the early Church set Wednesdays and Fridays as fast days prior to 70 C.E. During the fourth century, the Lenten fast was a part of the Church. The early Church fathers Origen and Augustine placed the importance of fasting with the actions of prayer and almsgiving.[5] Each of these disciplines should be toward God and not for gaining the attention of others.

It would seem that if the church is going to be a strong, vibrant, and Spirit led body of believers, fasting still holds a prominent place among other spiritual disciplines for our growth and development.

What is a Spiritual Discipline?

A spiritual discipline is a particular behavior or consistent habit undertaken for the purpose of maturing the believer. Studying the Scriptures through reading, memorizing, meditation and prayer in all of its varied forms, worship, serving others, celebration, chastity, fellowship, silence, solitude, submission, simplicity, giving, and communion are some of the disciplines that teach us about being a follower of Christ. Each in its own way provides strength for each day and understanding of the person and work of Jesus. These disciplines help to carve out space in our lives for self-discovery. They open the door for healing of wounds and restoration of mental and emotional health.

Fasting serves to help the believer open their heart and empty themselves before God. We cannot fast every day but we can incorporate it into our lives for designated periods of time then return to our normal pattern of eating. We are sure of the importance of Bible study to our Christian walk. In the same way it is important to investigate how fasting will strengthen our Christian experience.

WHAT FASTING SHOULD NOT BE

Entire books have been written on the subject of fasting and its purpose for Christians. It is important to understand that this discipline for spiritual formation is not a magic bullet. Fasting is not a way to lose weight under the guise of being spiritual. It is not for self punishment to get back into God's graces and it is not to get God to exact revenge on your enemies. Martin Luther said, "He wants nothing at all to do with you if by your fasting you court Him as if you were a great saint, and yet meanwhile nurse a grudge or anger against your neighbor."[6]

Jesus is not shy in warning His disciples about their behaviors. When it comes to fasting he tells them:

And whenever you are fasting, do not look gloomy and sour and dreary like the hypocrites, for they put on a dismal countenance, that their fasting may be apparent to and seen by men, Truly I say to you, they have their reward in full already.

Matthew 6:16 AMP

At another time Jesus uses a parable to dissuade the disciples from using fasting as a show of their religious superiority:

He also told this parable to some people who trusted in themselves and were confident that they were righteous [that they were upright and in right standing with God] and scorned and made nothing of all the rest of men: Two men went up into the temple [enclosure] to pray, the one a Pharisee and the other a tax collector. The Pharisee took his stand ostentatiously and began to pray thus before and with himself: God, I thank You that I am not like the rest of men—extortioners (robbers), swindlers [unrighteousness in heart and life], adulterers—or even like this tax collector here. I fast twice a week; I give tithes of all that I gain. But the tax collector, [merely] standing at a distance, would not even lift up his eyes to heaven, but kept striking his breast, saying, O God, be favorable (be gracious, be merciful) to me, the especially wicked sinner that I am! I tell you, this man went down to his home justified, (forgiven and made upright and in right standing with God), rather than the other man; for everyone who exalts himself will be humbled, but he who humbles himself will be exalted.

Luke 18: 9-14 AMP

In both passages the disciples are taught fasting is not to glorify the individual. Self exaltation will eventually lead to a downfall. Evidently, there is a right and a wrong way to fast. If your fast is to be acceptable it must begin from a heart that is hungry to know God and to hear from God. Fasting can turn the course of a family, a generation, or an entire nation but the motive has to be pure. These teachings from Jesus may have had their roots in the passage from Isaiah that tells us our motives have to be right or they will not produce the desired results:

Wherefore have we fasted, say they, and thou seest not? wherefore have we afflicted our soul, and thou takest no knowledge? Behold, in the day of your fast ye find pleasure, and exact all your labours. Behold, ye fast for strife and debate, and to smite with the fist of wickedness: ye shall not fast as ye do this day, to make your voice to be heard on high. Is it such a fast that I have chosen? a day for a man to afflict his soul? is it to bow down his head as a bulrush, and to spread sackcloth and ashes under him? wilt thou call this a fast, and an acceptable day to the LORD? Is not this the fast that I have chosen? to loose the bands of wickedness, to undo the heavy burdens, and to let the oppressed go free, and that ye break every yoke?

Isaiah 58:3-6

Fasting is not a tool for manipulating God. It is not to be used to lord your spiritual superiority over others. It is not a mechanical activity to rack up bonus points or to expect to receive things from God or as part of a checklist for "spiritual calisthenics." The Scriptures tell us a broken and contrite heart is what the Lord looks for in his people. (Psalm 51:17.) A consistent Christian life produces fruit that will remain. They will not try to be an overnight wonder or sensation. A life lived in the presence of God will simply continue to hunger for truth and more of the presence of the Lord in their life. Fasting helps draw us into the atmosphere of heaven.

DEVELOPING A FASTED LIFE

Each week has seven days. Each month has thirty or thirty-one days. Each year, with the exception of leap year, has three hundred and sixty-five days. In each week we have an opportunity to set aside a time for seeking God through fasting. If you have never fasted you might start by simply taking one day each week where you will miss one of your regular meals. With each progressive week you can remove one more meal from that day until you graduate to abstaining from food and liquids except water for an entire twenty-four hour period. At the end of a year you will have given the Lord an average of about 54 days of consecrated time. Although I have just outlined a helpful way for you to develop a fasted life, you should also pray and ask the Lord for His direction regarding fasting for your life.

In addition to not eating on a day of a fast, take the time to be still before the Lord. This may mean turning off any unnecessary sounds. You want to learn to hear the Lord's voice through your spirit and the distractions of computers, iPods, CDs (unless you are playing worship or instrumental music), and phones may interfere with your ability to hear the Holy Spirit. It is also helpful to limit your conversations with others as one of your objectives is to learn to quiet your mind and heart. On the day you fast, limit your reading outside of your work requirements to the Scriptures and other inspirational materials. Take every opportunity or set apart certain times during that day to spend time in prayer. If you are able, go to a park, your church if it is open, or a retreat center for a part of your day. When you are away from the mail and normal activities you move into an entirely different environment. It helps shift your heart and spirit toward the things of God.

As you grow in this discipline it will become a natural part of your spiritual armor. It will be a sweet time for you before the Lord. You will find that your sensitivity to the Holy Spirit will increase and your understanding of the ways of the Lord will mature. There may be times as you grow that the Lord will deal with you about adding additional time or giving yourself to an extended fast.

For those who have practiced fasting for a long time and understand the benefits, allow the Lord to stretch you even more. Begin to pray about fasting for specific nations, leaders of nations, or particular areas of concern in your community. It is easy to get overwhelmed by all the things facing us and our world but God can use one life surrendered to him to shift outcomes.

CAUTIONS

For seniors, nursing mothers, or anyone on prescribed medications, it is important to check with your healthcare provider before beginning a fast. It is also important to drink adequate amounts of water during the period of the fast. A few days before you begin an extended fast you may want to decrease your caffeine intake and slowly decrease the amount of food you ingest. This helps to prepare both your mind and your body for the fast. It is also helpful to begin to wean yourself from the excessive noises in your life. After you end your fast you may find the desire to remain in a quieter and calmer lifestyle.

CONCLUSION

There is no particular set of Scriptures that require fasting or contain an absolute command or law to fast. However, the scriptural references and the information found in Church history shows us the benefit of this practice as part of healthy spiritual formation. Cyprian, who served as the overseer of the Carthage church and one of the earliest leaders of the church wrote to a friend about fasting and perhaps this should serve as the benediction on the topic:

The one peaceful and trustworthy tranquility, the one security that is solid, firm, and never changing, is this: for a man to withdraw from the distractions of this world, anchor himself to the firm ground of salvation, and lift his eyes from earth to heaven... He who is actually greater than the world can crave nothing, can desire nothing from this world. How stable, how unshakable is that safeguard, how heavenly is the protection in its never ending blessings to be free from the snares of this entangling world, to be purged from the dregs of earth, and fitted for the light of eternal immortality.[7]

NOTES

[1] Craig Dykstra, *Growing in the Life of Faith: Education and Christian Practices* (Louisville, Kentucky: Westminster John Knox Press, 2005), pg.45.

[2] "Fasting." *dictionary.com* based on the (2010)Random House Dictionary. (New York: Random House, Inc. 2010). Retrieved May 20, 2010, from http://dictionary.reference. com/browse/fasting.

[3] Richard Foster, *Celebration of Discipline* (San Francisco: HarperSanFrancisco, 1988), pg. 55

[4] John Wesley, *Sermons On Several Occasions,* (London: Epworth Press, 1971), pg. 301

[5] Harvey Albert Smit, "Fasting: Guidelines for Reformed Christians" *reformedworship.org,* December 1987, Issue # 6. Retrieved May 20, 2010, from http://reformedworship.org/ magazine/article.cfm?article_id=120&id=6

[6] Robert Longman, Jr., "Fasting" *spirithome.com,* July 23, 2010. Retrieved May 25, 2010, from http://www.spirithome. com/fasting.html

[7] Cyprian of Carthage, "Epistles" *newadvent.org,* Epistle 1. Retrieved May 20, 2010, from http://www.newadvent.org/ fathers/050601.htm

Lane M. Holland, MSN, M.Div., was born in Atlanta, GA., accepted Christ as her Savior at the age of five, and has followed Him ever since. She is an ordained minister of the Gospel of Jesus Christ and currently serves as pastor of a developing and dynamic church that was planted by her senior pastor several years ago in Tucker, GA.

ABOUT THE AUTHOR

Germaine Griffin Copeland, founder and president of Word Ministries, Inc., organized in 1977, is the bestselling author of the *Prayers that Avail Much®* family of books. Her writing provide scriptural prayer and instruction to help you pray effectively for those things that concern you and your family and for other prayer assignments.

Germaine is the daughter of the late Reverend A. H. "Buck" Griffin, who served the Church of God (Cleveland, TN) as a bishop for over forty years, and Donnis Brock Griffin, Bible teacher and exhorter. She and her husband, Everette, have four children and eleven grandchildren. Their prayer assignments increase as great-grandchildren are born into the family. Germaine and Everette reside in Greensboro, Georgia.

MISSION STATEMENT - WORD MINISTRIES, INC.
Motivating individuals to pray,
Encouraging them to achieve intimacy with God,
Bringing emotional wholeness and spiritual growth.

You may contact Word Ministries by writing:

Word Ministries Inc.
Post Office Box 289
Good Hope, GA 30641

770.267.7603

www.prayer.org